PREFACE

Psalm 103:1-5 (RSV)

"Bless the Lord, O my soul, and all that is within me, bless His holy name! Bless the Lord, O my soul, and forget not all His benefits: Who forgives all your iniquities, Who heals all your diseases, Who redeems your life from destruction, Who crowns you with loving kindness and tender mercies, Who satisfies your mouth with good things, so that your youth is renewed like the eagles."

Just like the book of Joshua in the Old Testament where God provided for the needs of His people, II Joshua is a story of God's faithfulness to one little infant.

Baby Joshua endures one life threatening situation after another, but through these tribulations and trials, God's love and strength are fully displayed for all to witness.

II Joshua is a testimony to the power of prayer, the reality of support within the Christian community, and the abundance of grace and mercy our Heavenly Father bestows upon us. It is a story of miracles and blessings coupled with hope, as Joshua's journey continues during the writing of these chapters.

DEDICATION

John 15:13 (NIV)
"Greater love has no one than this, that he lay down his life or his friends."

On February 1, 1995 Joshua Mason Richardson received the gift of life. Although he does not know the identity of the donor, he does know that he has another family that is truly a part of him: physically, emotionally, and spiritually.

This book is dedicated to that family and to the infant who lay down her life for his; a total stranger who daily gives Joshua the breath of life.

Thank you and may God bless!

II Joshua

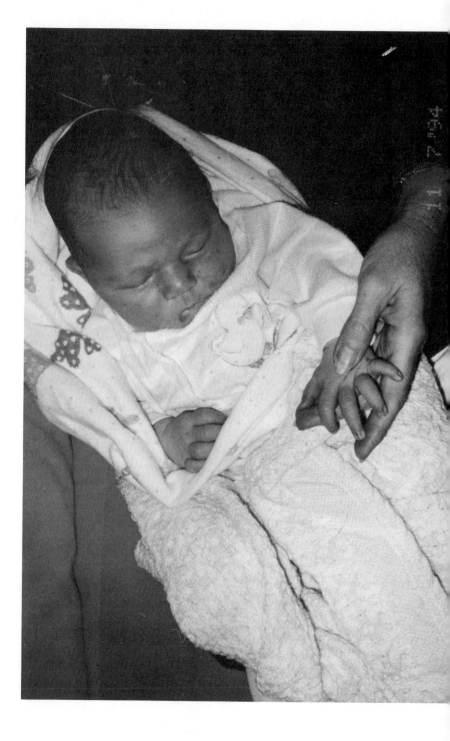

IN THE BEGINNING
CHAPTER I

Genesis 1:1-20 (RSV)
*"In the beginning God created the heavens and the earth
. . . the night and the day . . . the land and the sea . . . all the
living creatures . . . He saw that it was good."*

On November 2, 1994 at 6:42 p.m., God saw that it was good
and so He breathed life into 9 lb. 4 oz. Joshua Mason
Richardson, and ready or not, I entered the world.

I really had <u>not</u> given much thought to this next step of my
life. I was quite content where I was. My Mommy had taken
good care of me. She ate well, got plenty of rest, and exercised
to keep both of us in shape. I liked all the aerobics we did even
though sometimes the music got a little loud. Up until a month
ago, we went to work at the Savannah River Sight (a nuclear
facility) five days a week. "We" were in charge of hazardous
waste products. As a civil engineer, Mommy had lots of important duties to do, and as an aerobic instructor, she combined
her talent and energy to conduct a very challenging class that
was popular at the local YMCA. I helped. We had fun!

But then things began to happen. I almost made my grand
entrance a little too soon, and the doctor told Mommy to slow
down. No more trips to SRS and no more aerobics. Life became kinda boring for both of us. Daddy tried to keep up our
spirits by playing with us when he came home from his work at
SRS. He's a computer technologist. I recognized Daddy by his

big warm hand when he placed it on Mommy's tummy. I'd kick him to say hello. We guys have to stick together.

So day after day, for two long weeks we waited. Mommy got really swollen, Daddy got really anxious, and I got really big. And then as I was getting used to this "rest and take life easy," I suddenly was tossed, turned, pushed, pulled, shoved, and at last, born.

THE BEGATS

CHAPTER II

Joshua 24:15 (NIV)
". . . But as for me and my household, we will serve the Lord."

Before I was born, Mommy and Daddy tried to decide on my name. A pretty standard procedure, but did you ever think about the great responsibility of naming someone? What if I didn't like my name? I heard them discussing their choices-- Erica, Christina, Marie, even Alexa. They're all girls' names. I'm a boy! I was happy when they settled on Joshua Mason. Mason is in honor of my Daddy, and Joshua, which means "God saves" or "Savior" in Greek, is the only name Mommy even considered for a boy since she liked it so much. No question about it, I definitely am a Joshua! Of course, we had no way of knowing how much we were going to rely on God saving me as the days progressed.

Physically I am my own unique blend of Mommy's family and Daddy's family. My big brown eyes (I hear most babies are born with blue or gray eyes) come from my Great-grandma Bittler. My dimples look just like Daddy's. My curly hair can be traced to Mommy and Daddy because they both have lots of curls. The beautiful auburn color of my hair comes from my Great-grandpa Clark who was killed almost 50 years ago in World War II. Only Granny & I have this special hair color and actually Granny's getting a lot more gray as she celebrates her 50th birthday this

14

week.

✳ ✳ ✳ ✳ ✳

I was born into a family with a strong Christian heritage. Nana, my deceased great great-grandmother, was the matriarch of Mommy's family. Nana begat Great-grandma Jean who begat Granny who begat Mommy. I have an Aunt Tammi married to Uncle Mike and an Aunt Sandi, an Uncle Hoss and another Uncle Hoss (actually Mommy's twin brothers, Ronnie and Robbie. They call each other Hoss.), and a Gramps and a Great-Grandma Bittler. On Daddy's side, I have a Grandma Kay and a Grandpa George, an Uncle Randy married to Aunt Debbie, an Aunt Lynn married to Uncle John and two cousins--Galey and Daniel.

As regular, Bible-reading, born again Christian church- goers, both sides of my family rely heavily on God's direction in their lives. Nana set the example on Mommy's side. She was the first woman elder of her Presbyterian Church back in 1932. She inspired Granny to become active in the church, mainly the mission field, traveling to places like Jamaica, Brazil, and Cuba. My Uncle Randy is studying to become a minister, and has spent many years working with Campus Crusade for Christ.

I'm glad I will be brought up knowing Jesus, and that God is my Heavenly Father.

NOVEMBER 16, 1994
CHAPTER III

John 14:1 (KJV)
"Let not your heart be troubled: ye believe in God, believe also in me."

After two days in the hospital, I'm ready to go home. I'm all rested up from being born and want to get on with what happens next. I've mastered sucking, sleeping, dirtying my diapers, and even a short cry now and then. I've been weighed, measured, circumcised, and checked by doctors and nurses.

Daddy seems ready to roll, but poor Mommy's a little under the weather. She says it's hard for her to sit down and her legs are still swollen. She moves slower than I remember and we aren't doing anything strenuous like aerobics. Granny drove down from Mercer, PA to help us settle in for the first week. I think she came just to take my picture. Every time I look at her all I see for hours is a red dot. But we're adjusting quite well. Even Tasha and Chelsie--my two cats--seem to enjoy having me around, although I came as a surprise to them. I'm not sure they know who or what I am. Hey, I'm Baby Joshua.

I like this baby stuff. There are all sorts of toys for me to play with. At the moment I'm not too interested, but in time I'm going to be like other babies--grabbing the bright colored rattles, hugging the stuffed animals, chewing on the blocks and balls and assorted music boxes. And, check out my new wardrobe. Wow! I think they were expecting two or three more of me.

Everything is so soft and warm. I like cuddling up in my clothe
and blankets.

I have my own room. No joke. With a crib and all sorts o
things like a night light and a monitor. The monitor is so if I'r
alone and I need help someone will come running at my sligh
est whimper. **Great**. The first night I don't need it because
sleep with Daddy and Mommy. They put me in an old cradl
that was my Gramps'. The Amish back in Mercer refinished :
completely so it looks better than it did fifty-two years ago.
can't quite get used to my new surroundings, so I keep everyon
awake most of the night. No big deal. I'll sleep all day.

Night number two at home finds me in my own room wit
Granny sleeping in a spare bed next to me. (She still has tha
camera!) I'm wondering if I'll be in a different room every nigh
of my life. Silly family. All night long Granny checks on me an
changes my diaper pretty frequently. I hate having my legs lifte
up. I cry, but she keeps on doing it every time she decides
need a clean diaper. At least she notices that my legs are coc
and puts a few more receiving blankets over me.

Mommy comes in to see if I'm hungry. I really am starved
but nursing wears a guy out. A few good swallows and I'm bac
to sleep. I ignore Granny when she tickles the bottom of m
feet to keep me awake. **Not interested.**

❆ ❆ ❆ ❆ ❆

If they expect me to continue to get my beauty rest, they ar
going to have to be quieter. What is all this commotion? Grann
seems worried that she smells something in my room--like natu
ral gas. Mommy and Daddy are calling the landlady to see
there is a possible leak. After several hours of people in an
out, the leak is found, fixed, and all the frantic concern is begir
ning to wane. I think it was one big overreaction, but maybe
just don't grasp the significance. Time for a little more mil
and a little more sleep.

I hear Granny repeatedly tell Mommy how good I am. "If an
of the five of you were this good, your father and I would hav

had ten more of you." "I've never seen a baby so good." "Joshua never cries." "He's only five days old and already he sleeps through the night." "How can you be so lucky to have such a good baby?"

Don't look now, but I may just get so I like being up on this pedestal! According to Granny, I'm the best baby in the world. And she swears she is <u>not</u> prejudiced. I believe her.

❋ ❋ ❋ ❋ ❋

Hard to realize seven days have come and gone and that I'm now a full week old. Granny is leaving to go back to Gramps and Great-grandma Bittler. Mommy seems a little stressed, but Granny reassures her by reminding her that I am the best baby ever. Finally our little family of five (including the cats!) is on its own. This is the beginning of a wonderful, exciting life together. It's kinda like sink or swim, and believe me, we're way past the doggie paddle! We are going to be just fine.

I manage to continue to keep everyone on their toes. After all I'm still the center of attention. We sleep when I sleep and we eat when I eat. I'm doing my best to help Mommy and Daddy be less set in their ways. They like to sleep when it's dark and be awake when it's light. Not me--I like the opposite. I hope they adjust soon because I don't like Mommy waking me up all day long.

Then something strange happens. It's hard to describe all I'm feeling but I know I'm in big trouble. I hurt everywhere. I cry. Mommy changes my diaper. That just makes it worse. My legs ache. I can't breathe right. My chest hurts. I continue to cry. Mommy and Daddy take turns trying to figure out my problem. I'm telling them the best I can. They're getting upset with me. "Hey guys, I'm in pain." More tears. Now Mommy's crying too. I'm really sorry. No, I don't want to be fed and I don't have to burp and I'm not fussy. Remember me. I'm Joshua-the best baby Granny ever saw. I'm crying because I'm in real trouble.

Finally it's morning. I'm so tired all I can do is whimper.

"Please, please help me." Mommy talks to Granny and Grann thinks maybe I should see a doctor. Mommy calls, and th nurse wants to know my temperature. Mommy gets the ther mometer but after a few minutes she realizes that is hasn't move above 95 degrees Farenheit. She calls the nurse back. Th nurse suggests she try again with another thermometer. I ca tell Mommy's scared. But she obliges the nurse not once, bu twice. These are not ORAL thermometers.

They all concur--my temperature is way below normal. I coul have told them that. My skin is cold and clammy. I hope some one figures this out soon, because I'm losing interest in what' happening. I hear Mommy leave a message on Granny's an swering machine. "Something's really wrong. I'm taking Joshu into the doctor's office. Please pray that I'm just a bad mothe and don't know how to read a thermometer yet."

The trip to the doctor's office is a blur. My body's numb an I'm confused. This isn't what I expected life would be like. Thi is awful.

We don't stay long at the doctor's office. Immediately she ha us follow her to University Hospital. There I am pumped full c antibiotics because their best guess is that I have bacterial men ingitis. I sure hope they're right 'cuz I'm not liking this ver much.

It doesn't take long for the doctors to realize I'm not respond ing correctly to the medicine. They start checking for othe things. They x-ray me, poke me, check my eyes, and generall annoy me. I'm too tired for these procedures. I wish they woul leave me alone. I guess they've never been this sick.

Before I know it, they put me in an ambulance and transfe me to a second hospital. Mommy's crying. I want to stay witl her, but I'm whisked away from everything I'm familiar with. don't know any of these people. I don't think I want to.

This new hospital is the Medical College of Georgia (MCG) Maybe only really, really sick people come here. I'm not sure But I think I'm really, really, really sick.

The next few hours are the worst yet, but finally Mommy and Daddy are told that the diagnosis is a coarctation of the aorta. BIG words that mean nothing to me. Dr. Ken Murdison continues to explain that once (and if) they stabilize me they will do heart surgery on me. First thing tomorrow, they will fix the artery going to my heart.

It seems that babies are born with a "hole flap" in their hearts and when the hole closes--as is normal procedure--the heart must pump harder. My hole closed last night, but my heart couldn't pump the blood because my artery isn't right. It needs to be fixed. There are three different ways to do the fixing. One is to use an artificial plastic piece. One is to use my own vein from my arm. I can't remember what the third option is. When Dr. Victor Moore operates tomorrow, he'll decide what to do when he sees my exact problem. Okay by me.

Now that I think about it, I guess I cried when I was changed because I wasn't getting any blood flow to my legs, and I instinctively was telling anyone changing my diaper about my pain. No one figured it out. Nor did Granny pick up on the fact that my legs (the doctors call them lower extremities) were cold to the touch. Now they're saying I was <u>so</u> good because I didn't have the energy to cry or even to eat. I think they're going a little too far with that explanation. I was good because I have a sweet temperament and a wonderful disposition. I still do!

I want to see Mommy and Daddy again soon. It's been hours. The doctors have put IV's in my arms and my groin and my head. They have me wired to many beeping machines. I'm secured so that I can't move at all. I hurt everywhere.

Oh, where's Mommy?

It's time to be wheeled into the operating room. I know I won't remember any of the actual surgery, but even getting me prepared has been traumatic. I certainly am glad that soon we can put this day behind us and go on with our normal lives.

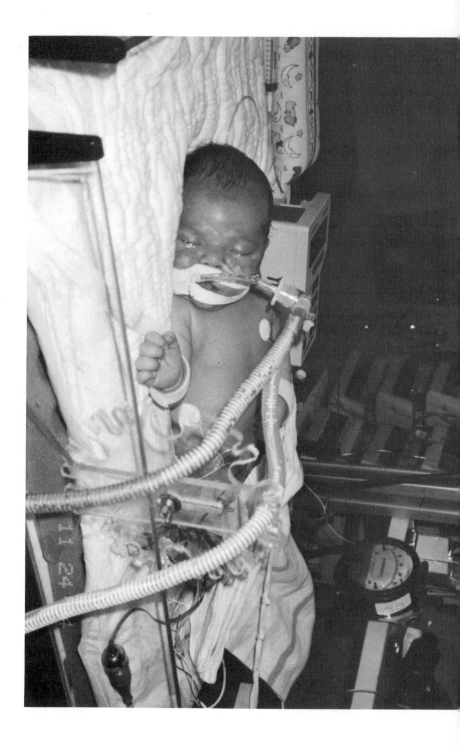

THANKSGIVING

CHAPTER IV

Philippians 4:6-7 (RSV)
*"Have no anxiety about anything, but in everything by prayer
and supplication with thanksgiving let your requests be made
known to God. And the peace of God, which passes all understanding, will keep your hearts and your minds in Christ
Jesus."*

The days after my surgery are filled with pain, tears, and
anticipation. I have the physical pain. Mommy has the tears.
We all have anticipation. Dr. Murdison and Dr. Curtis Steinhart
try to keep me comfortable with many sedatives. I know they
were expecting this to be a routine repair of the aorta with no
complications. Actually maybe they weren't expecting it as much
as Mommy, Daddy, and I were, but I can tell you we want this to
be history soon 'cuz we have big plans. Plans that do not include ventilators, heart monitors, blood transfusions, IV
feedings, or doctors, nurses, and hospitals. We are going to
have a wonderful Thanksgiving AT HOME with most of my aunts
and uncles on Mommy's side whom I've yet to meet. There will
be Aunt Sandi, Uncle Hoss, Uncle Hoss, and even Gramps and
Granny. Mommy already has the turkey and all the fixings for a
great meal. Of course I will only get it second hand since by
then I should no longer be fed IV and will be nursing again.
Daddy's family will be there too. We are going to have fun.

The first step to getting home for the holidays is to get me weaned off my ventilator. No disagreement from me. I hate having this tube down my throat. Granted it breathes for me and granted I'm weak from the surgery, but don't let anyone tell you that being on a ventilator is anything but awful. Have you ever breathed through a straw? Try it.

The first time they "extubate" me--which means they pull the tube out of my lungs, (Notice how I picked up the medical jargon!)--I'm able to breathe for only five minutes before I go into respiratory arrest. I'm not ready to do this alone quite yet. A big discouragement. Back goes the tube, but the doctors agree that it is quite common to fail the first time. **Whew!! I thought I did something wrong.**

I once again must be sedated. The doctors think I'll pull the feeding tube out of my nose if they don't keep me "asleep." **Right on.** But living my life sedated is no picnic either. However this is just to be for one more day. Good thing because this Thursday is Turkey Day and remember we have plans. Aunt Sandi is flying in from New York City. She works for the NBA and doesn't have a lot of free time. She's expecting me to be home so we can play. And the Uncle Hosses both are taking vacation days from their jobs to come meet me. Uncle Robbie "Hoss" will also be flying to Augusta. He works for a private company in Columbiana, Ohio as a mechanical engineer. I hope I don't get him confused with my Uncle Ronnie "Hoss" who will be driving down from Cockeysville, Maryland where he is a civil engineer for the Maryland Department of Transportation. Mommy says that I should be able to tell who's who even though they are identical twins.

I'm also going to meet my Gramps for the first time. He'll drive Granny. Before leaving on their trip, Granny ties a blue ribbon on the old hickory nut tree in the front yard. She will leave it there until I leave the hospital. A lot sure has happened since I saw Granny thirteen days ago. I know she's been concerned since she calls the hospital to talk to Mommy anywhere from four to ten times a day. I think she calls for lots of reasons--to support Mommy and Daddy, to hear how I'm doing, and to tell Mommy about all the people praying for me. They've been praying faithfully, not just during my surgery, but even during my recovery. I'm grateful. I have a really good feeling that I'll breathe on my own for good this time.

❋ ❋ ❋ ❋ ❋

Twelve hours. I breathed by myself for twelve hours before "crashing." Respiratory arrest is what the doctors call it. I'm bummed. Mommy and Daddy are bummed too. Now it looks like I'll have to spend my very first Thanksgiving in the Pediatric Intensive Care Unit (PICU) because no one wants to extubate me again for at least four more days. The doctors say I need a little more time to get stronger.

I don't know how they expect me to get stronger when I have so many tubes and wires and interruptions. The monitors beep and the nurses take my vitals and the doctors make their rounds and the intercom continually spews requests of one kind or another. If it weren't for all the medication I'm on, I wouldn't be able to get any rest at all. But the morphine and fentanyl do their thing. I think I should share my medication with poor Mommy and Daddy. They look so tired, and I don't think the doctors are giving them anything. Even though Daddy brings Mommy home for five or six hours each night, I don't think they are getting much sleep. I hear them say how many people call and leave messages on their answering machine and how they feel obligated to return the calls. And I know they cry a lot. I wish I could reassure them.

❋ ❋ ❋ ❋ ❋

Only two people are allowed in PICU at a time to visit patients. No food allowed. No flowers allowed. No spending the night (at least no beds) allowed. These are the rules.

My Grandpa George and Grandma Kay come and visit. Usually they come in my room one at a time accompanied by Daddy or Mommy. And Uncle John stops by to see me when he's making his rounds. He's a security officer right here at MCG. I feel much safer knowing he's around. Aunt Lynn comes by but my cousin Daniel isn't allowed in because he's too small. Funny thing is he's a lot bigger than I am. I guess there aren't any "too small" patients. Forgive my grumbling, but I wish I were too small for heart surgery, too small for ventilators, and too small for PICU!

Today is the day before Thanksgiving. I am going to get lots of company. The nurses make an exception to the rule and let Mommy bring Granny and Gramps in together. I hadn't realized I was looking so different from three weeks ago, until I saw Granny's eyes fill with tears. She left Mommy's side and let go of Gramps' hand to come touch me. (Of course everyone had already "scrubbed" so there would be no germs going from Granny to me.) She put her hands on my head and prayed for me. Her silent tears were quickly absorbed by my receiving blanket.

Out of modesty, I haven't mentioned that I lay naked on blankets which protect me from getting too hot from the heating pad that keeps me warm. I guess Granny didn't realize I would be very pale and motionless and have tubes literally out of every hole in my body and be hooked up to a half dozen monitors. She was visibly shaken which obviously upset Mommy. But Gramps--meeting me for the first time--was stoic and in control. Good thing. He's a guy. Someday we'll go fishing together. But not now.

For now I'll spend my first Thanksgiving in the hospital. I'm glad the nurse finally laid a diaper over me. I suppose actually putting it on would be too uncomfortable with my foley catheter (another medical term!) attached. Holiday or not, the doctors need to keep a close eye on my urine output. It doesn't look like I'll be getting to eat any turkey but, at least, I am meeting all my relatives on Mommy's side, except my Aunt Tammi and Uncle Mike. Since they both are medical doctors, they have to work today in Pittsburgh, Pennsylvania. We'll miss them, but right now I'm just trying to get acquainted with everyone else. One at a time I meet them: Uncle Ronnie, Aunt Sandi, Uncle Robbie. They each tell Mommy how pretty I am and they look at my scar from my surgery. They seem surprised that I'm so small. Mommy reminds them that she didn't think I was small at all while I was being born. I guess you can tell none of them ever had a nine pound four ounce baby.

I'm a tad bit offended when I hear the plans for the rest of the day. The holiday dinner at home has been cancelled. The turkey went back into the freezer. The Bittler-Richardson family is going to the Sheraton Inn for a Thanksgiving buffet. Only one member has not been invited. ME. I can tell no one wants to leave me, but two by two they come and let me know that they'll miss me, but will return in a few hours. I've heard that family tradition was scrapped this year when everyone decided to come to Georgia. For the past twenty-five years Granny and Gramps have cooked the turkey and had the family together in Mercer. I'm honored to know that I'm important enough to change such a long ritual. I plan on revamping everyone's lifestyle--for the better--as soon as I recover. I don't want to be taken for granted.

❋ ❋ ❋ ❋ ❋

I can envision the actual meal. Lots of food. Lots of conversation. Lots of fun. Lots of thanking God for His grace and mercy during my operation. Lots of gratitude that I'll be home soon and maybe a little sadness that I'm not there right now.

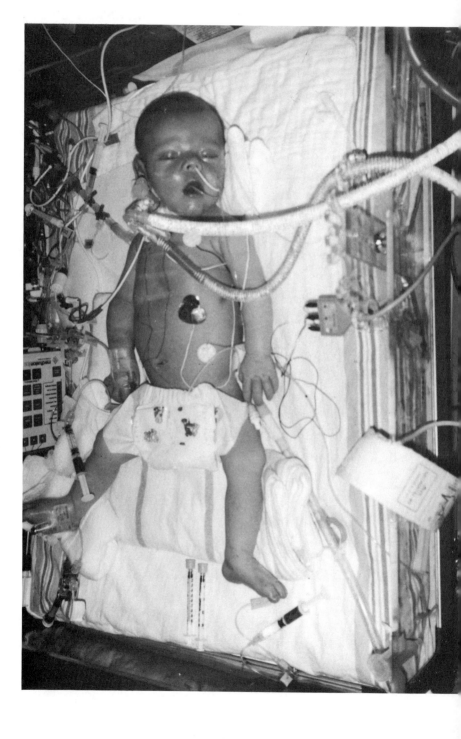

GOD'S MESSAGE

CHAPTER V

Romans 8:31 (RSV)
"What then shall we say to this? If God is for us, who is against us?"

Granny says that hospital waiting rooms are often dreary and sad, but filled with expectation. I guess that is true. I've never had the opportunity to experience that side of a hospital stay. I'm always right in the middle of the action. But I do know that Mommy and Daddy often eat and sleep in the waiting room and that all my relatives have spent many hours there. I know they are anticipating my recovery.

Granny says waiting rooms are good for something else. Everyone in a waiting room is going through a temporary crisis--some more major than others. Everyone is powerless to control the situation which makes waiting rooms excellent places to pray. Granny believes people pray a lot--which is a good thing.

So, when Granny isn't in my room watching me, she sits in the waiting room and prays. But today something special happened while Granny prayed. I know it happened because she told me about it. She said she was crying and worrying about me and she felt as though her heart was breaking into lots of little pieces. All of a sudden God told her that He would not take me Home. I guess no real words were spoken, but Granny said she knows our Heavenly Father laid that message on her heart. "I will not take Joshua."

Then her tears flowed even faster. Soft, warm streams. She said even the tears were different. Those were (and still are) tears of joy. Granny seems so much happier. She calls it the "Peace that Passeth Understanding." Until I hear her telling Mommy and Daddy and Gramps, I was thinking it would be our little secret. She explains that not everyone will understand, but she will share her joy with our brothers and sisters in Christ.

Mommy presses Granny for details. I think we all want the security of knowing how soon things will go back to normal. Will my heart and lungs soon be strong enough to sustain my life without the ventilator? Will I recover quickly with no side affects from the surgery, medicines, or oxygen? Granny says only God knows all the answers. He is in charge. Out of His mercy and kindness He shared the message "I will not take Joshua." Nothing more. Nothing less. He will give us the courage and strength to hold on. And, according to Aunt Tammi and Uncle Mike, we're headed for a roller coaster ride. Lots of ups and downs. I think each one of us is looking for an UP. Maybe things would be better if we get on the Merry-Go-Round for a while. Going in a circle might be a welcome relief!

❈ ❈ ❈ ❈ ❈

Days come and days go. Mommy's family goes back to their homes. The sense of urgency remains. I cannot breathe on my own. The doctors seem confused by my inability to recover. The nurses are overwhelmed by my fragile condition. The level of frustration continues to build.

In order to gather more information about my condition, the doctors do a heart catheterization. The procedure is very hard on me and I have a difficult time before, during, and after. The diagnosis of a hypoplastic left ventricle in my heart does not sound good. There is a way to correct such a condition which entails three surgeries (called the Norwood Procedure). I'm not thrilled at the possibility. I can tell Mommy is upset. She tells

Granny by phone about the latest turn in events. Granny says we must have faith that God will protect me. The faith of a mustard seed can move mountains.

Two days later, when the diagnosis is reversed, there is much jubilation. Mommy nicknames me Mt. Joshua and we all know God gets the glory.

So, here's the deal. My heart seems to have recovered from the surgery quite well. The problem seems to be solely my inability to breathe without help.

Dr. Steinhart tells Mommy that there are several options. 1.) Give me more time. If all goes well, I will be weaned off the ventilator and breathe on my own. 2.) Give me several experimental--oops, can't use that word around insurance companies. I mean, unconventional drugs that will help my lungs do their thing. 3.) Keep me on the ventilator and maybe go home with a breathing tube. 4.) List me for a heart/lung transplant. 5.) Turn everything off and see how I respond.

He says he is cautiously optimistic although he admits that I am puzzling him. He refers to me as a glass that the optimist will call half full and the pessimist will call half empty. He thinks our family likes the half full concept.

※ ※ ※ ※ ※

The roller coaster ride continues. The monitors record my many ups and downs. There are moments of encouragement but nothing we can look at as a break through. Now we hope I will be home by Mommy's birthday--December 5th. It's getting harder and harder to look at the glass and think it's half full. Each time we think there is improvement, it never materializes.

A typical day goes something like this. Daddy calls my room first thing every morning before he goes to work. The nurse gives him my condition, including temperature, weight, respiratory rate, pressure in my heart and lungs, and how I slept. He tells Mommy, who starts getting ready to come see me. He then leaves on his hour drive to work.

The nurses change their shifts in the morning, so the new

nurse takes all my vitals, gives me my medicines (I'm taking six at the moment!), and draws blood. I'm being fed IV so I also get my breakfast before Mommy comes. She continues to pump her milk for me everyday and freeze it. Someday soon I hope I'll be able to eat normally again.

Granny calls the nurses' station every morning to get her update. At around ten o'clock she calls again to talk to Mommy. They visit a little, but the conversation mainly centers around me.

I am sedated almost all of the time. The nurses keep vaseline on my eyelashes to keep my eyes from opening and drying out. I get morphine for pain. I'm attached to so many machines that it's impossible for anyone to hold me. I know Mommy longs to cradle me, but no more than I yearn to be cuddled. We're both being brave.

I have some get well cards hung up on my door and a balloon or two. Everything else in the room is "hospital stuff."

Mommy and Daddy have requested that no visitors be allowed in the room so that I may rest and stay germ free. It also gives them a chance to catch their breath. It must be hard for them to try to continue with any sense of normalcy in their lives.

I can hear Mommy visit with the nurses and talk to the doctors during their rounds. She has many questions and often the doctors only have a few answers. All afternoon Mommy sits by my crib. Praying, watching the monitors, talking to Granny and other people who call. Daddy comes as soon as he can after work. Three times a week Mommy leaves for two hours to teach aerobics while Daddy keeps me "company." The rest of the evenings both Daddy and Mommy stay until 9 or 10 p.m. Granny calls before she goes to bed, and every night she reminds the nurse to tell me she loves me and is praying for me. Also Daddy never goes to sleep without calling and saying goodnight. Tomorrow it will begin again.

God willing.

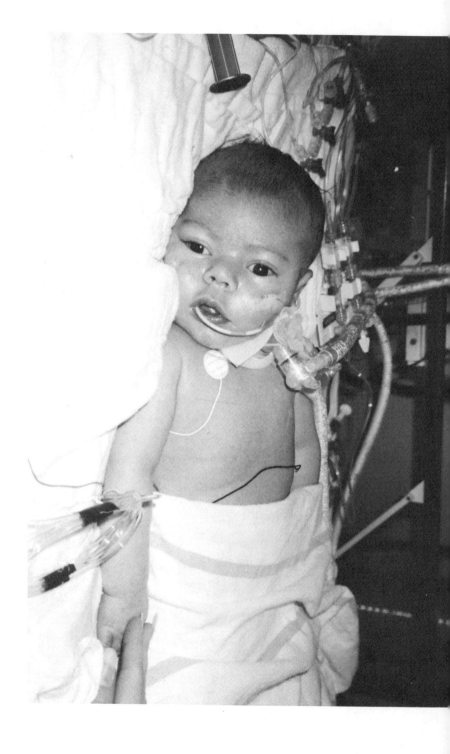

PRIMARY PULMONARY HYPERTENSION

CHAPTER VI

Philippians 4:13 (RSV)
"I can do all things in him who strengthens me."

Mommy's birthday comes and I'm still not out of the woods, nor the PICU. To keep Mommy from becoming too discouraged, some of my nurses decide to help me give her a card. They put finger paints on my hands and feet and together we make her a wonderful gift. I think she's having mixed emotions. Kinda happy yet still sad. Will she ever get to bring me home? I'm already four weeks and five days old. I want to be treated like a real baby. I want Mommy to hold me and cuddle me.

Dr. Gene Fisher, Dr. Tony Pearson-Shaver, and Dr. Ed Truemper have been consulting with Dr. Steinhart and Dr. Murdison. They are going to try a different approach. They are going to use prostaglandins to help me. It's not as conventional as the direction we've been going, but my oxygen requirement has increased and there is concern that I may have a condition called Primary Pulmonary Hypertension (PPH). That's really bad news! Usually the high pulmonary artery pressure, which occurs with the coarctation of the artery, corrects itself after the heart surgery. With PPH, the pulmonary pressure remains too high in the lungs and the heart cannot maintain the extra effort necessary to pump the blood through the lungs for the oxygenation. Worst of all, PPH has no cure. Of course there's hope

that I have another form of pulmonary hypertension--one tha
responds to prostaglandins.

There's some talk about moving me to another hospital ir
South Carolina where they specialize in prostaglandin treat
ments but my condition is not stable enough for the trip. That':
okay with me. I don't want to go too far north since I'm a south
ern gentleman and this is winter. I certainly want to stay clos:
enough so I can be home for Christmas.

Actually I don't hear too much being said about my gettin;
home for Santa's visit at all. Everyone seems pretty weary o
this situation. We take one day at a time. I'm not improving.

Dr. Robert Introna (the anesthesiologist) has been asked t:
check out a very experimental procedure that involves a ga:
called nitric oxide. Not to be confused with laughing gas--ni
trous oxide. This will hopefully bring the pulmonary pressure:
down from my lungs. Medical College of Georgia has neve:
used this before, but we get more daring as the days turn int:
weeks.

Dr. Steinhart's first option of "Give Joshua more time. If al
goes well, he'll be weaned off the ventilator and breathing or
his own" is history. His second option of "Give Joshua severa
unconventional drugs" is at its decisive stage. Nitric oxide i:
the final choice left to us. If this doesn't work, I guess we'll go t:
option number three.

Meanwhile, I'm having other problems. I've come down witl
a bacterial infection called serratia so now I'm taking antibiot
ics. Also, I've had several other medical emergencies that hav:
been the result of faulty equipment or human error. Each time
my Heavenly Father has gently delivered me from the evil tha
could have consumed me. Daily, He gives my family the strengtl
to continue.

Mommy says she can get her hopes up no longer becaus:
each time she does, there is another disappointment. I feel th:
same way. Instead of getting a stocking full of toys this Christ
mas, I am going to receive a tracheotomy. Now if that isn't a bi;

disappointment I certainly don't know what is!

Protocol at MCG dictates that long term ventilated patients receive "trachs." It is also the consensus of opinion I'll be better without the breathing tube going past my fragile vocal chords. My feeding tube still will remain through my nose going directly into my stomach. I'm gaining some weight. I wish I could say I'm thriving, but then I'm certain I would be accused of gross exaggeration or morbid humor. However, everyone is grateful that I'm showing some signs of progress physically.

So Christmas comes and goes. So does New Year's Eve and New Year's Day. We don't celebrate much, but we daily thank God that we have each other. Existence is a struggle. But God is faithful to give us the strength to help us continue.

On January 6, fifty days after my initial surgery, Dr. Steinhart stops in my room for a visit. Granny is also visiting for a few days, and she and Mommy listen carefully as Dr. Steinhart explains how options one and two didn't work. We're all trying to rack our brains to remember option number three when he drops a bombshell. He thinks we should go to option number four. Since I'm still totally sedated, on the muscle relaxant, norcuron, morphine, nitric oxide, and who knows what else, I don't react at all. But Mommy and Granny do. Mommy has lots of questions but already she's late for her aerobics class. They can't exercise without their teacher. She meets Daddy in the hall as she dashes out. Tears flow.

The diagnosis is Primary Pulmonary Hypertension.

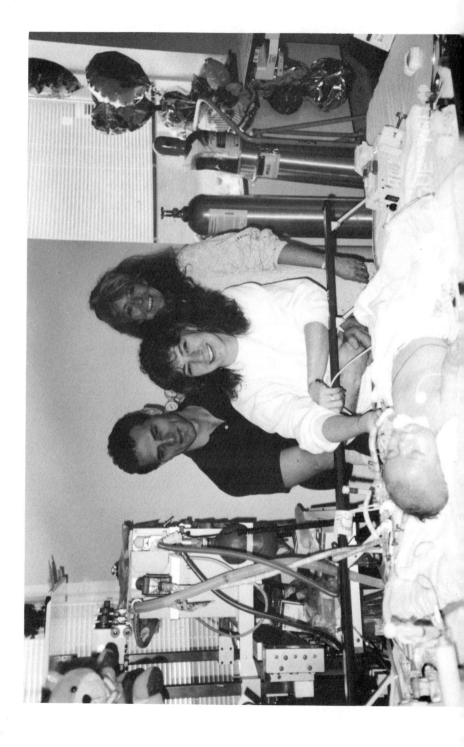

THERE'S NO WRONG DECISION
CHAPTER VII

Psalm 46:10 (NIV)
"Be still and know that I am God."

How come we skipped option number three? Why don't
we try option number five? Why are we considering option
umber four?

I don't think any of us ever for one minute really considered
.sting me for a heart/lung transplant. It was just something we
put in the very back of our minds, knowing that if my medical
ondition deteriorated to such an awful state, we had one last
litch measure we could grab. Is Dr. Steinhart saying that we've
eached that final stage? No wonder everyone is crying.

I remember Mommy and Granny talking before my heart sur-
:ery about donating my organs if I didn't make it through the
operation. I was so sick then that I really didn't care. But they
:ried, and I know Mommy told Dr. Murdison that he was to do
:verything possible to save me but if God took me Home that
:he wanted as many sick babies as possible to have the Gift of
Life. Now, maybe my life depends on a family going through the
oss of their baby.

Daddy looks numb. Granny's left to call Aunt Tammi and
Jncle Mike one more time. Except for calling me about six
.imes a day when she's in Pennsylvania, I think she calls Aunt
Tammi and Uncle Mike the most. They have been wonderful
:xplaining as much of the medical jargon as they know and

then researching whatever else is necessary so that Granny, Mommy, and Daddy are fully informed.

Granny's daily phone calls become more than routine. She has become dependent on them. Each day she calls not just me, Aunt Tammi and Uncle Mike, but also Great-grandma Jean, Aunt Sandi, Uncle Ronnie, and Uncle Robbie. She keeps that whole side of the family updated each and every day. Gramps says he is hoping to buy stock in the phone company so he can recoup some of the many dollars Granny spends daily. Granny is oblivious to his concern.

This time Aunt Tammi is at the hospital delivering a baby. So Uncle Mike patiently walks Granny step by step through transplantation. He explains that it is not a "cure all," and that there are lots of problems. But with a diagnosis of PPH, that may be our only solution left. The decision must be Mommy's and Daddy's.

When Mommy returns from aerobics class no one is feeling much better. Dr. Steinhart comes into my room again to talk about option number four. Maybe we will just have one lung transplanted. It's almost impossible to receive a heart/lung at my age. Premature babies' lungs are not developed enough to be any good for me and hearts are in short supply and will go to heart patients. That doesn't sound too encouraging.

Option number three--send me home with the ventilator--is still possible. But with PPH it will not cure me--only give us some time out of the hospital. Option number five--just stop everything--most likely will result in my dying sooner rather than later.

Just like Uncle Mike, Dr. Steinhart stresses that the decision is ours to make. "There is no wrong decision." If Mommy and Daddy take option three, we may live happily for days, weeks, or months. If they take option five, "we" may not live very long together, but no one can predict the future. Both options three and five require nothing more of Dr. Steinhart or MCG. I will be discharged immediately.

However, option number four will require the staff to stabilize me, transfer me, and most of all find a hospital that will accept me as a transplant patient. Dr. Steinhart gives Mommy and Daddy some time to decide what to do in a situation where the doctors feel there is no "wrong" decision and we feel there is "no" decision.

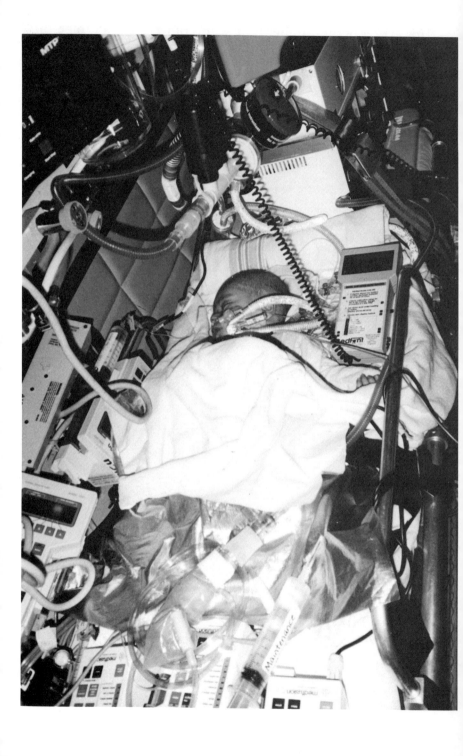

FLYING TO PHILLY

CHAPTER VIII

Revelation 3:7-8 (KJV)
"And to the angel of the church in Philadelphia write, these
things saith he that is holy, he that is true, he that hath the
key of David, he that openeth and no man shutteth, and
shutteth and no man openeth, I know thy works: behold I
have set before thee an open door."

I guess you can call me naive. I thought once a transplant
was needed, the patient waited until a donor was located and
presto--good as new. That doesn't seem to be my case.

Since the Medical College of Georgia does not do transplants,
I will have to be transferred to another hospital. That in itself is
going to be quite a challenge. Nitric oxide is so new that no one
seems to know how it will react to the change in pressure in an
airplane. I hope it doesn't inflate my lungs like a helium balloon and cause me to float to the ceiling. That might freak
Mommy and Daddy out.

The doctors continue to say I'm not stable enough for a long
flight. Matter of fact, these last few weeks I've been having
"spells." I can't explain it and the medical staff doesn't understand either, but I occasionally need to be "bagged" (hand ventilated) in order to breathe. It's very scary and unpredictable.
When this happens, my ventilator is set to 100% oxygen and my
nitric oxide is increased and the doctors suction me (which I
hate) and often I'm given morphine and more norcuron. I even-

tually stabilize, but I wonder what's causing these episodes.

Aunt Sandi, Daddy, and Granny are having a conference call with a top surgeon at Children's Hospital in Boston. After the call, Granny seems depressed. Their request of having me transferred there has been rejected by the doctor because of my size, age, and medical condition. Donors for an infant heart/lung transplant are almost impossible to find. This surgeon suggests a single lung transplant; however, he cannot justify the time and expense on a baby with such pre-existing medical problems. He all but tells them it's hopeless. Now I'm feeling a little depressed too.

Anyway, I never wanted to go to Boston. I know that I really want to go to Children's Hospital in Pittsburgh. After all Aunt Tammi and Uncle Mike are doctors in Pittsburgh, and Granny and Gramps live only sixty miles away. They can visit and maybe we can live with them if need be. Definitely Pittsburgh is my first choice. Imagine my disappointment when they also refuse to accept me as a patient.

Come to find out most of the hospitals are rejecting me. I had no idea that I wouldn't be wanted everywhere--or anywhere! Dr. Steinhart puts my condition into a computer internet. Only three hospitals respond. Children's Hospital of Philadelphia (CHOP), St. Louis, and Loma Linda in California. Dr. Steinhart rules out Loma Linda immediately because of its distance. I'm too fragile to go that far. The decision comes down to CHOP or St. Louis.

Mommy and Daddy pray for direction from God. They look for answers by calling both hospitals. They get information on the transplant teams. They talk to a family whose son has received a double lung transplant in St. Louis. The family reports their satisfaction in both the surgeon and the follow up care at St. Louis. One glitch, however. The surgeon, Dr. Thomas Spray, has left and is now in Philly. That makes the decision harder. Heads it's Philly. Tails it's St. Louis.

Meanwhile, Granny also is praying for an answer. Within

days she's feeling a strong leading toward Philadelphia. Her decision is threefold. 1.) The Church at Philadelphia in the Book of Revelation is the church God is most pleased with. 2.) She prays with a member of the Billy Graham ministries for me, and as Donna prays, she inadvertently misspeaks, asking God to intervene and bring me to Philadelphia--when in reality the request was for Pittsburgh. Granny interprets that not to be a mistake, but a leading. 3.) While talking with a family member of a Cuban friend, the woman encourages Granny to bring me to the hospital where she works. Believing it is in Miami, Granny asks the name of the hospital. University Hospital of Philadelphia is the reply. Probably any one of these incidents is enough for Granny, but all three must be Divine intervention.

So Mommy and Daddy flip the coin: Heads. Philadelphia!

❋ ❋ ❋ ❋ ❋

Dr. Steinhart explains that MCG is not in the business of keeping chronically ill patients alive. Therefore, now that we have a decision--transplant--and a destination--Philadelphia-- we must prepare to leave. It takes us just nine days. During this time, Dr. Steinhart is in constant contact with Dr. Spray and his transplant staff.

The doctors agree that I will not be a candidate for heart/ lung, but rather lung (or maybe double lung) and that Dr. Spray and Dr. Nancy Bridges, my new cardiologist--who will be arriving in Philadelphia from St. Louis one day after me--will check my heart but not replace it. Dr. Spray and Dr. Bridges have performed half a dozen or so similar operations. I will have the distinction of being the youngest baby ever to receive a lung transplant.

I also will have the dubious distinction of being the first patient to be transported by airplane on nitric oxide. Dr. Pearson-Shaver and Kathy Thomas, the transport nurse, will be in charge of my travel arrangements. They practice emergency situations on me, preparing for the trip. It's a good thing I'll be completely sedated and won't know what's happening. Daddy and Mommy will be on the air-ambulance with me. I think they are hoping to be sedated, too!

The nurses throw us a party to say good-bye. I'm not actually invited, but I hear all about it. It's been almost eleven weeks that I've been here. Seventy-five days. But who is counting? I haven't been held, cuddled, or barely moved for seventy-five days. I haven't taken a bath, eaten by mouth, or breathed on my own for seventy-five days. I haven't burped, swallowed, or coughed for seventy-five days. My liver and spleen are extremely swollen--full of blood. I'm on no less than 70% (sometimes 100%) oxygen. I have a high white blood count, low SATS, high pulmonary pressures, fever, and am bleeding from my trach. No wonder I'm not invited to the party. I'm a mess!

Everyone is praying for my safe trip to Philadelphia. Yesterday at 2:30 p.m. my ventilator quit. The nurse noticed immediately and within one hour I had a brand new one. As usual, I know God was watching over me. If the ventilator "died" during the plane trip--no matter how much Dr. Pearson-Shaver and Kathy prepared--I would die too. Now we don't need to worry about that.

✳ ✳ ✳ ✳ ✳

It's January 30th. My big travel day. I'm strapped on to my stretcher. Feels strange. The clothes, I mean. I'm dressed for the first time in seventy-five days. I hope what I'm wearing is appropriate for travel. It doesn't look in vogue to me. I sure don't see anyone else with aluminum foil on his head. The idea behind the aluminum foil is to keep my body temperature stable. The nurses say it's cold up north in Philadelphia. I wouldn't know. It was warm Georgia weather on November 15, 1994 when I first came to the hospital.

But much has changed in seventy-five days.

The trip to the airport goes well. Uncle John drives the police cruiser, using the red light with Mommy riding "shotgun" and Daddy in the back seat. I follow in the ambulance behind them.

Once we arrive, Daddy checks out the air ambulance while Dr. Pearson-Shaver and Kathy secure me on the stretcher. It's a small plane, but it has a pressurized cabin which is imperative for my condition. When we plug in my brand new ventilator and it doesn't work, we are all grateful we remembered to bring the back up battery pack.

The pilot, who only an hour before flew the plane from Louisiana to Bush Airport in Augusta, Georgia, tells us we should be in Philadelphia in about one and one half hours. It's hard for me to believe that I'll soon be one thousand miles from home.

✳ ✳ ✳ ✳ ✳

In three more days, I will turn three months old.

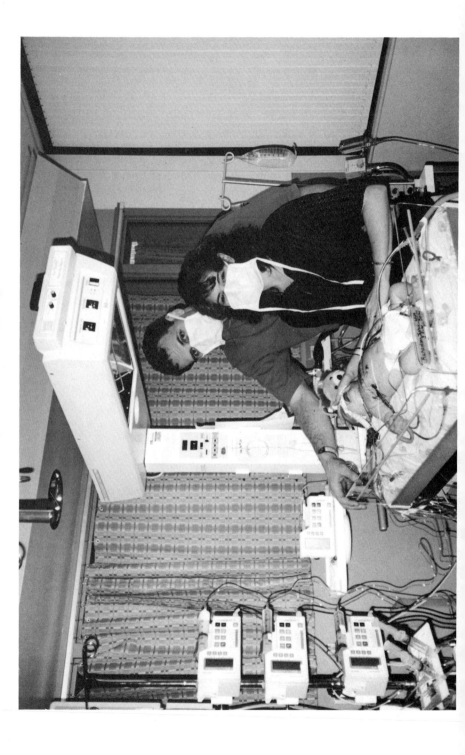

MIRACLE WITHIN 24 HOURS
CHAPTER IX

Matthew 19:26 (NIV)
". . . With man this is impossible, but with God all things are possible."

We're all so grateful that the nitric oxide worked perfectly during the flight. Matter of fact, everything went fine. Saying goodbye to the transport team was the only hard part.

Mommy called Granny in tears. CHOP is so big compared to MCG that it's overwhelming to her. From my perspective, it doesn't seem much different. One ICU room looks pretty much like another one even though I was in the Pediatric ICU in Georgia and I'm in the Cardiac ICU here in Philadelphia.

The medical director of the CICU, Dr. Gil Wernovsky, officially welcomed me to CHOP, but I haven't met the chief cardiothoracic surgeon, Dr. Spray, because he's in California for a conference. Dr. Bridges doesn't start her new job until the day after tomorrow, but the transplant coordinators explain that I'll start the necessary tests tomorrow to get me prepared to be listed as a candidate for a new lung or possibly two. I'm wondering how many more patients are waiting ahead of me. From all we've heard it could be a long wait. I'm sure it's going to be very stressful.

We discover right away that CHOP has strict visiting hours-- and there are times I can have no visitors at all. These times coincide with the changing of the nurses' shifts. Mommy and

Daddy must leave me everyday from 3-4 p.m., 7-8 p.m., an
11-12 midnight. Also, no one is allowed in my room from 5:3
a.m. until 8:30 a.m. Mommy is not pleased, but she obeys th
rules.

So, at 7:00 p.m. both Mommy and Daddy take their sui
cases and hail a cab, leaving me alone, while they check in a
the Philadelphia Ronald McDonald House. That will be thei
home away from home for as long as it takes. And I guess th
CICU will be my home away from home--at least for the tim
being.

My first night in Philadelphia is completely uneventful, a
though there are definitely some adjustments that will have t
be made. I know that Granny isn't able to make her nightly ca
into my room to tell me that Jesus loves me and so does she.
think she said that's the top adjustment on her list. And Dadd
and Mommy are having problems getting to and from the hos
pital without a car.

✳ ✳ ✳ ✳ ✳

As a new day dawns, we have important business ahead c
us. Today I am being assessed for my status of being a cand
date for a lung transplant and that means I have to show ther
I'm really sick, but that I'm also strong enough to handle th
waiting, the surgery, and the recovery. Now that sounds a littl
contradictory to me, but what do I know about this whole mess
I'm grateful I'm here at all.

There are two transplant coordinators--Barb Sands an
Jeanette Engro. They have decided to list me as a candidat
after reviewing my charts and doing some tests. The brain sca
found fluid around my white matter. The results of the bloo
tests for AIDS, epstein barr, and CMV will be available tomo
row. That's also when I'll meet Dr. Spray and Dr. Bridges.

Mommy and Daddy have spent a lot of time filling out form
and giving everyone my insurance information and other im
portant data. They even had blood tests done themselves. Nov
there are phone calls that need to be made, reassuring friend

and relatives that we arrived safely and are adjusting as well as can be expected with a sick baby (me), a new city (Philadelphia), and a change in weather (snow!).

As soon as Dr. Spray returns from California he drops in to say "hi" to me before we all go to bed on this our first full day at CHOP. I like him immediately. He's soft-spoken, well-dressed, and seems very mellow. I really like the way his compassion mingles with his confidence. I know he is a well educated, dedicated leader in the relatively new field of lung transplantation in children. Aunt Tammi told Mommy that lungs have only been transplanted in the last three to five years. The success ratio continues to increase--that's good news--but not many babies have had this surgery. Just by looking at Dr. Spray, I can tell he and I are gonna be a successful team.

❊ ❊ ❊ ❊ ❊

February 1, 1995 starts out like every other day since I've been hospitalized. Mommy and Daddy come first thing in the morning. I'm still sedated the majority of the time. My many medicines are given IV. My food is pumped to my stomach through a nose tube. I'm on all sorts of monitors. I'm looking forward to Dr. Spray examining me to evaluate my condition. Today I meet Dr. Bridges for the first time.

At 2 p.m.--less than twenty-four hours after I am listed as a transplant candidate--Dr. Bridges comes and tells us a donor has become available. ALREADY!! The lung(s) will be mine as long as it is disease free.

Immediately a sense of urgency fills not only my room, but my entire world. My life. This is really going to happen. I am really going to have a transplant.

With all the hustle and bustle of moving me from Georgia to Philly and the confusion of getting settled into our new surroundings, I'm not sure any of us actually gave the transplant itself much consideration. I thought that Dr. Spray would examine me and re-examine me, and maybe decide that we really didn't need this drastic procedure after all.

I'm learning that most of what I thought is wrong. At one day shy of my three month birthday, I'm getting an education on organ transplantation that is up close and personal. Wow! will officially be the youngest lung transplant to date--make that double lung transplant because they have decided to give me both of them.

From 3:00 p.m. to 7:00 p.m. a whirlwind of activity over whelms me. But three thoughts appear that I will never forget First, the words Granny told me more than two months ago "God will not take Joshua Home" stayed in my mind. I know that God is Truth. He is my Creator, His Son is my Savior, and His Holy Spirit is my Protector. Therefore, I will fear no evil.

Second, I think of the power of prayer. I am well aware of the fact that many, many people are praying for me, and that these prayer warriors have been faithful, daily petitioning God on my behalf. I know that as the decision to forge ahead with aggres sive treatment was made that the prayers became more intense and frequent. The prayers always were lifted up in God's will I know God answers prayer.

Third, I think of the baby whose lungs I will receive. Since lung transplants are based on size, I know that a family is expe riencing the tragic loss of their own infant. A family we will never meet--because those are the guidelines established--has in its own grief been unselfish enough to think of someone else That someone is me. What a humbling experience.

The donor is an eight month old girl who is brain dead from a tragic, unexplainable auto accident right here in Philadelphia Usually transplants must be retrieved and flown to the recipi ent. In my case, we are only floors apart.

At 7:00 p.m., I am wheeled into surgery.

At 11:00 p.m., I am wheeled out of surgery.

Mommy makes the observation that I look like I just fough Mike Tyson and lost. But in reality, I won an even bigger battle The battle for life.

What a difference twenty-four hours makes.

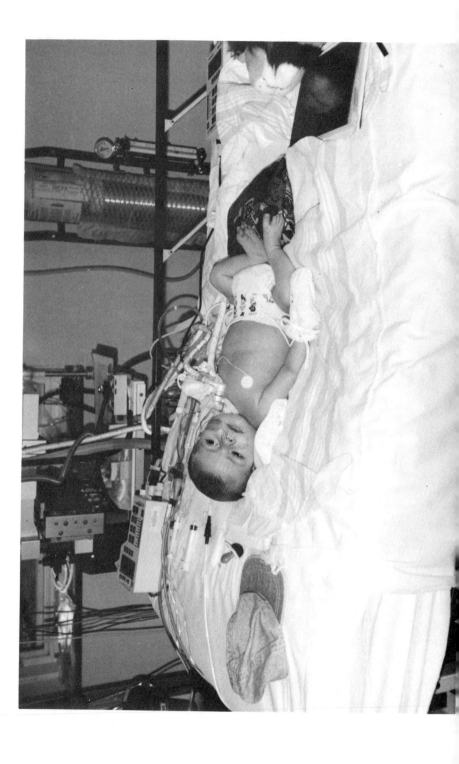

A PATIENT'S PATIENCE
CHAPTER X

Romans 5:3-4 (NIV)
"Not only so, but we also rejoice in our sufferings, because we know that suffering produces perseverance; perseverance, character; and character, hope."

Granny decided only a few weeks ago to start keeping a journal on my progress, her observations, and whatever else she feels like writing. Her entry for Thursday, February 2, 1995 starts out, *"Happy three month birthday, Joshua. Good things always seem to happen on Wednesdays for Joshua. He was born on a Wednesday, had his heart repaired on a Wednesday, and now has received his new lungs on a Wednesday. Let Jesus Christ be praised. The song, 'When Morning Gilds the Skies' flows from my lips. I am feeling very privileged to be a part of this unbelievable miracle. I share with Traci what a blessing we are experiencing, being participants in this painful yet amazing time. It reminds me in some small measure of how Mary and Joseph might have felt, and I am really overwhelmed by God's graciousness and goodness. I am certainly feeling unworthy, but oh so grateful."*
In subsequent entries Granny describes such things as her drive three days after my transplant to Philadelphia in a major snow storm (so Daddy and Mommy can have a car), and her reaction upon first seeing me. She also keeps track of many statistics registered by my monitors. They seem so important now--just like all the pulmonary pressures and heart pressures

56

monitored in Georgia--but as I continue on my road to recovery, the numbers become a blur and the only real indicator of my progress is me. If I do say so myself (excuse my lack of humility), I am quite an excellent source to rely on.

When I received my new lungs, Dr. Spray put a few stitches in my heart and also closed the trach site in my throat. I'm still breathing with the help of a ventilator, but within four days of my transplant, I am showing enough progress that the doctors are ready to extubate me. AGAIN.

Tried this before. Wish I could say, "Been there. Done that." But the truth is that I've "been there. Didn't do that." Those were my old, gray, very sick lungs. These are my brand new, pink and healthy lungs. I'm ready!

Everyone marvels at how beautiful I am without the tubes. They are only half as excited as I am. I have no breathing tube down my throat. I no longer need to be suctioned (which is that awful procedure where the nurses shove a small plastic suction device down my breathing tube to "suck" secretions out of my lungs--which are a result of using the ventilator in the first place.) I'm breathing by myself for the first time in twelve weeks, and although it looks very labored, I am so happy. I can move without too much pain. I'm still attached to monitors, two chest tubes, and I have a line going into one of my arteries for easy access for blood draws, but I can squirm and wiggle and best of all--soon Mommy can hold me.

This being a baby is starting to feel good again. I can forget about the fact that both of my feet look like pin cushions from all the needles. By putting booties on my feet, we can all ignore that. I'm not worried that I can't make any noise when I cry. The nurses watch me to know when I'm upset. No one seems overly concerned that my eyes don't seem to focus and kinda float here and there. My huge scar (a small case w) will be hidden when I start wearing some of my brand new clothes. Actually I think I may have outgrown some of my clothes without having worn them even once. But that's a great sign.

Then all of a sudden, without much warning, I begin having difficulty breathing. A chest x-ray reveals my lungs are cloudy. My blood gases have poor results and after twenty-seven hours of freedom, I once again must be put back on the ventilator. The explanation: I "tuckered out." The fact that I have not been breathing on my own for twelve weeks caused my muscles to weaken. No one thinks I'm in rejection or have an infection or anything major like that.

Of course Mommy is very discouraged. Daddy, too.

But in four more days, we're ready to try again. And this time things go really well for nine full days.

Then on February 19th I have many symptoms that cause the doctors to be alarmed. I'm running a fever of 102 degrees Fahrenheit, my blood gases show too much carbon dioxide, my SATS are too low, I have lost one and one half pounds, and I cry inconsolably so that everyone knows we're in trouble. I even remove my own chest tube to let them know just how uncomfortable I am.

Thank God that my x-rays show no signs of rejection. Dr. Spray has decided against a biopsy because that is a very invasive procedure and could possibly cause my lung to collapse. So instead, a culture is taken from my newly placed breathing tube and we wait to see if any "bugs" grow.

We don't have to wait even twenty-four hours for a Gram Negative Rod B to appear. NOW we will do the biopsy. We must know if my body is rejecting my new lungs.

I'm taken early in the morning to the operating room. Since I'm sedated, Mommy and Granny go to the hospital cafeteria for lunch. We've started a new routine this week. Daddy spends Fridays through Sundays in Philadelphia and then flies back to Augusta to work. Granny spends Mondays to Fridays here and flies back to Mercer for the weekends. Mommy stays with me always. This is Tuesday. Daddy's at work. Granny's visiting. Mommy's here.

I don't handle the biopsy well. My lung collapses and a new

chest tube must be inserted. My kidneys aren't functioning properly. My face is swollen from the fluid build up. I'm cold and clammy to the touch. I need blood because my hemoglobin is low and my white count is high. My chest x-ray shows there is fluid around my left lung. If the result of my biopsy indicates rejection, at least we've caught it early. I guess that makes all this suffering worthwhile.

※ ※ ※ ※ ※

When Dr. Bridges first comes in my room, I can immediately sense a problem. Oh, no--I must be in rejection. Imagine my shock when she tells Mommy and Granny that the bad news she is bringing isn't that I'm in rejection. Rather it is the fact that somehow the tissue they collected was lost. We have NO results. How could something so important and so difficult to obtain end up missing?

It's a toss up as to who is the most upset. Dr. Bridges, Dr. Spray, Mommy, Daddy, the nurses, Granny, or me.

This just heaps one more frustration upon a mounting list. Mommy is gradually reaching her limit of staying calm during these human errors. In the past week there have been half a dozen or more "mess ups"--forgetting one of my feedings, giving oral medication through my tube, letting medicine run out of my line, not using sterile procedures at the appropriate time, and accidentally allowing all the milk Mommy so diligently pumps each day and freezes for my future use to thaw, necessitating throwing it away. Mommy cries.

Now is the time to call upon the Lord. Because if we've learned anything from this, we've learned that God is in charge. Humans make mistakes, but God is our refuge, our strength, and our hope.

RONALD MCDONALD HOUSE

CHAPTER XI

Hebrews 13:2 (KJV)
"Be not forgetful to entertain strangers: for thereby some have entertained angels unawares."

When Mommy and Daddy aren't in the CICU with me, they are at the Ronald McDonald House (RMH). I haven't had the opportunity yet to see where they are staying but I know they are grateful such a place exists.

Several of the other patients on my floor have their parents staying there also. I hear it's a big house that looks almost like a castle. It's three stories high with beautiful ornate wood carvings along a winding staircase. Mommy's room is on the second floor. It's large with a queen size bed, a bureau, a rocking chair, and a night stand. There's one closet and one window. A construction crew works from 7 a.m. to 4 p.m. everyday right outside the window, preparing for a new addition.

For one week Mommy, Daddy, and Granny all stayed in the one room, but now that Daddy and Granny are doing their alternating routine, there's only two in the room at a time.

The RMH is set up to help serve families during their time of crisis. There are fifteen to twenty rooms available now, but as soon as the addition is done, there will be lots more rooms. For $10.00 a night, the families staying at the RMH get room and board. Volunteers usually make dinner and often serve it to the guests. The kitchen is open and available to everyone all the time. For the most part, the bathrooms must be shared, along with household chores which are assigned to each family. There is a large play area for the kids--whether they be patients or siblings--and there is an outside playground. Of course with all the snow and freezing winter weather, no one uses the playground at this time of year.

There is definitely a family atmosphere. Smaller family units exist within a larger family structure. Volunteers drive a donated van several times a day to and from CHOP. During the five to ten minute ride, the passengers often talk to each other about their children's progress or lack thereof. Somehow, chronic medical problems such as mine and all the kids whose parents stay at the RMH, seem to bridge any socio-economic gaps that might exist. Everyone is suffering. Some worse than others. Some babies get better. Some don't. Some even die.

Today is one of those days with me where things aren't awful, but could certainly be a lot better. My x-rays continue to look hazy. I have a slight fever, diarrhea, and I feel very uncomfortable. The new tests they did on my lungs show that I have poor compliancy. I think that means that my lungs are stiff.

Dr. Spray is thinking about doing another biopsy. I barely feel recuperated from the first one. As the doctors discuss the pros and cons, we get the results of a stool sample saying I have rotavirus. Not a big deal for a healthy person, but it's potentially dangerous for a little tyke like me--one who is on cyclosporine daily to suppress my immune system. No wonder I'm feeling lousy.

Over the next eight days I am treated for the rotavirus, for rejection (with three large doses of steroids), and for withdrawal when taken off all morphine, but I am not weaned one bit from my ventilator. A fellow could become discouraged, but, during this same time frame, I meet my Aunt Tammi and Uncle Mike for the first time. I think they're pretty cool and I can tell they think I'm great.

Two other exciting things happen. I cut my first tooth and

Mommy gets to HOLD me. We've waited so long! It's absolutely the best feeling, even though we have to work around the ventilator and feeding tubes and all sorts of wires and lines and monitors. To be cradled in arms that love me and to know that I'm safe and secure is a pleasure I can't describe.

I know this is the first step toward my eventual recovery. I look forward to being discharged from the hospital and staying with Mommy at the Ronald McDonald House during my recuperation. That's what happens when the doctors discharge you. They send you to the RMH while you continue to improve. Only one major problem I still must overcome. I'm still on the ventilator. Dr. Bridges explains I may have to receive a trach again.

Oh, no! Can this be history repeating itself, or will I soon be a guest at the Ronald McDonald House?

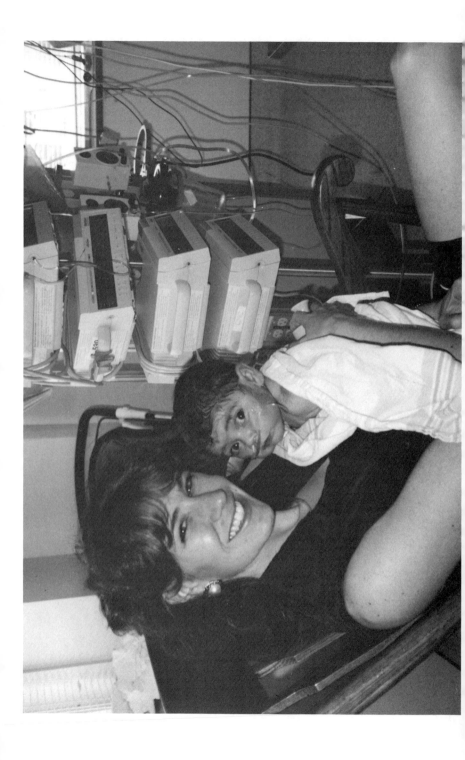

FREQUENT FLYER MILES

CHAPTER XII

Isaiah 40:31 (KJV)
"But they that wait upon the Lord shall renew their strength;
they shall mount up with wings as eagles."

A month has come and gone since I received my lungs. Granny leaves today and Daddy comes. I'm glad he's here for my second biopsy. We celebrate the good news that there is no sign of rejection or infection. Unfortunately there is some bad news. I will be put in an iron lung to help my breathing. The same type of iron lung that was used years ago for polio victims. Daddy comforts Mommy who is feeling discouraged.

If I weren't so upset by the circumstances of this iron lung thing, it might seem a little humorous. Kinda like the stepsisters in the fairy tale, Cinderella. The first stepsister tries to stuff her huge foot in the glass slipper and she can't get it on. The second one's foot is way too small for the slipper. That's how the iron lung experience is for me. The first iron lung we try is way too small. I'm squeezed in it and it is very uncomfortable. The next size larger is way too big. It sucks me through the hole. There's no way this is going to work.

But, to my surprise, the doctors have one more option to try. It's a VERY sophisticated ventilator called the SERV 300. It costs about $20,000 and they borrow it from another unit. The concept sounds great. I do the breathing. When I get tired out, it will automatically breathe for me. It measures tidal volume.

Just one more number for Granny to record daily in her journal. If all goes well, I should be weaned in eleven days.

With the weekend over, Daddy flies to Augusta and Granny returns from Mercer. Gramps now wants to buy not only AT&T stock, but also stock in the airlines Daddy and Granny fly.

Today, Granny's plane is late because it had to be de-iced before take off. She decides to take a taxi to CHOP to make up some of the lost time. During the trip, she starts talking to the driver, Geráld. He seems so genuinely interested in my condition that Granny shares her faith with him. He is a dedicated Christian from Haiti and he offers to pray for me. A mutual respect quickly turns to a friendship and from this day on, Granny will go to and from the airport by taxi. Geráld will take her.

The remainder of the week is fairly uneventful. I have some fluid drained from my left side. My chest x-ray is still hazy. My ECHO seems normal. I'm moved from an isolet into a crib. Each day my tidal volume is turned down slowly but surely. Daddy comes back for the weekend. Granny leaves.

Mommy begins taking an aerobics class. It appears to me that everyone is settling into a routine. I guess it's my responsibility to liven things up. What better way to get attention but to extubate myself? Only thing--I still can't breathe, so I'm happy that Dr. Lenny hears the beeps and comes to my rescue. I hadn't realized that this little episode would put me back to almost square one with the SERV 300 or I would have tried something else for attention.

❇ ❇ ❇ ❇ ❇

Granny's back. Must be a weekday. My bronchoscopy shows no narrowing of my windpipe. The pulmonary function test shows some improvement. The fluid in my chest cavity has been determined to be chyle (a fatty substance) from my lymph system and not from my lungs. My upper body is bright red for some unknown reason, but I quickly turn blue when the night nurse accidentally bumps the heating element while emptying

he tube to my ventilator and disconnects my oxygen supply.
m surprised to see Granny "flip" when the exact same thing
appens with my day nurse. Both times I'm immediately
bagged" and respond well. Better than Mommy or Granny.

❈ ❈ ❈ ❈ ❈

I have visits from my Aunt Sandi, Uncle Hoss, and Great-
randma Jean.

❈ ❈ ❈ ❈ ❈

I'm still "eating" with a nasal gastric (NG) tube every other
our. Mommy has finally, after four months, given up saving
ne her milk. The stress of our situation didn't help matters.

❈ ❈ ❈ ❈ ❈

I am moved into a new room because there are two new lung
ransplant patients. One is a two year old boy and the other is
. twelve year old girl. I'll be sharing my nurse with one of them.

❈ ❈ ❈ ❈ ❈

I recently became aware of a unique problem lung transplants
ose. Lungs are the only transplanted organ with access to the
utside world and germs. How? By breathing.

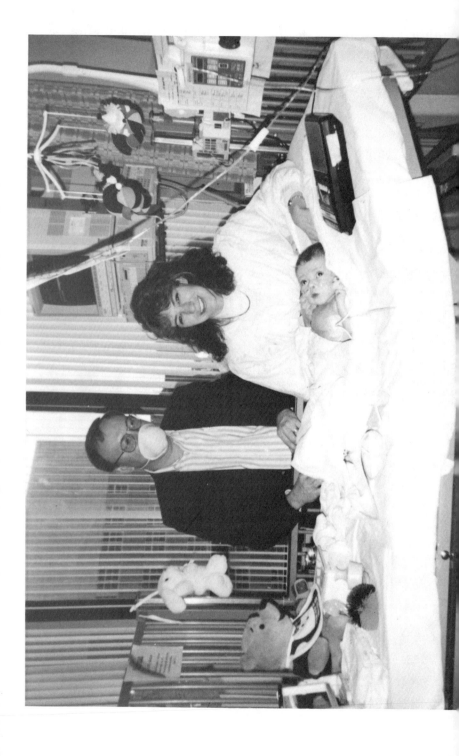

OUT OF CHOP

CHAPTER XIII

Romans 12:12 (RSV)
"Rejoice in your hope, be patient in tribulation, be constant in prayer."

Progress has been made.

Granny's journal entry on March 15, 1995 states, *"It continues to hold true that good things happen to Joshua on Wednesdays. At 1:45 p.m., Joshua was extubated. Now, three hours later he seems content and peaceful in his little oxygen tent; sucking his pacifier and holding it in by himself with the backside of his right hand. His left hand and arm have his arterial line in them and are outside his plastic house. Joshua is receiving 60% oxygen and another medicine in gas form to help open up his airway, so that he can breathe. His SATS are 100%, his temperature is 36.4 degrees Centigrade, his blood gases look good, his heart rate is 142, his cyclosporine level is 256. He gets lots and lots of people in to check him, encourage him, and listen to his lungs. Some just come to look. He is a miracle."*

Within a week I'm out of the tent but continue to receive oxygen by wearing a nasal cannula. More progress is made. I'm dressed for the first time in four months. Mommy gives me my first real tub bath. I also get to sit in an infant seat in my crib. I now have my own physical therapist, speech therapist, and occupational therapist. Not to mention some different tests. I've had a neurological test, an eye test, and a cranial ultra sound. I think my "vacation" is over!

Mommy's former minister and Granny's present ministe[r] from Mercer comes all the way to Philadelphia to meet me an[d] to bring Mommy a check from Granny's Sunday School clas[s]. We appreciate their generosity and his willingness to come s[o] far. It's fun having a visitor even though I barely see his fac[e] because he must wear a mask to protect me from germs. I'[m] still in a semi-sterile environment.

On March 29, (of course, it's a WEDNESDAY), after taking [a] crash course on how to insert my NG-tube in order to give m[e] my medicine and also feed me (it's very complicated since if i[t] accidentally is in my lungs and not my stomach, I'll drown o[n] formula), how to give my oral medicines, how to use the oxyge[n] tank and all my many monitors, how to dress a sterile sight ([I] still have a broviac line in my heart), how to do physical therap[y] and how to properly put me in a car seat to keep me safe, w[e] are discharged. WHEW!

Mommy's overwhelmed. Granny's overworked (carryin[g] equipment, toys, medicines, diapers, and clothes). I'm over[-] joyed. After eight weeks in Philadelphia's hospital (who's count[-] ing?), I'm going to the Ronald McDonald House.

WAIT. Wait just one minute. I'm not wearing that silly mask over MY face. You guys put your masks back on. Wha[t] do you mean that it's impossible to have everyone we wal[k] past on the way to the car wear a mask? I don't want thi[s] mask on. I'm scared. If you think I'm sitting all alone in [a] car seat the very first time without someone holding me please think again. I'm terrified.

Where's Dr. Lenny? Each night he would come and hol[d] me and rock me and we would watch Jeopardy and Whee[l] of Fortune reruns. Where are my musical mobiles that Dr[.] Jonathan cranked up for me repeatedly? Where are all the tapes I listened to with lullabies and Bible songs?

Mommy, what's going to happen now?

GEORGIA ON MY MIND

CHAPTER XIV

Luke 7:50 (KJV)
". . .Thy faith hath saved thee; go in peace."

Our first night at the Ronald McDonald House is not easy. We get a bigger room than Mommy's first room. We are on the third floor, with three beds, a table and chairs, a crib and musical swing for me, and our very own bathroom. We are in isolation. Except to dash down to the cafeteria, no one leaves the room. Except for the home health nurse, no one enters the room. There are no exceptions for me. I stay put.

My nasal gastric tube clogs, my SATS drop, I need oxygen, and I don't sleep well because I'm not adjusted to my new surroundings. Other than that, everything is peachie keen. Oh, yeah--one more thing. I cannot tolerate the cyclosporine in my mouth. It makes me gag. I'm not being stubborn, it tastes awful. So, I refuse to swallow it.

Mommy and Granny take turns staying awake with me. I still have no voice so someone must watch me to see if I'm getting upset. I try to be good, but occasionally I must let them know I'm not getting all my needs met. Actually I'm allergic to the formula they are giving me--it makes me have awful tummy aches--but it takes awhile for the experts to figure out why I'm irritable. Sure would be a lot easier if I could communicate more effectively.

After being at the RMH for two weeks, Daddy visiting on weekends and Granny during the week, I get a really nice surprise. It's Easter and the Bittler clan (minus Aunt Tammi and Uncle Mike who will be working) are all coming to Philadelphia to celebrate the resurrection of our Savior with me.

The doctors have seen me several times as an outpatient and think I will do just fine out of my room, but not too close to any people. So we have a nice picnic on the campus of the University of Pennsylvania while most of the students are gone for the holiday. And I visit the motel where everyone is staying and I go to the Liberty Bell and Independence Hall (staying outside at both places). It's fun and I hate to see the weekend come to a close.

I wish Mommy and I were flying back with Daddy. I miss Chelsie and Tasha. I miss my room and my toys. I miss the warm weather.

Up until last week, Mommy was on medical leave from her engineering job. But due to downsizing and my continual health problems, she was advised to take voluntary separation. So now when we finally return to Augusta (which I hope is soon) I'm gonna have a full-time, stay at home, best Mom in the world Mommy!

❋ ❋ ❋ ❋ ❋

I continue to spend the vast majority of the days in my room at the RMH. Except for going to the hospital for check ups, things are pretty dull.

My check ups are irregular. Sometimes everything looks good. Sometimes we have problems. Sometimes my anti-rejection medicine (cyclosporine) is not in the approved range. Lately I've been having blood in my stools. I even spent a night at the hospital for observation, but wasn't readmitted to the CICU. I guess that means my condition is improving.

One week shy of spending six full months away from home, we get the approval from Dr. Bridges that we had been hoping and praying for. We can leave Philadelphia and drive back to Augusta. It will be a long, fifteen hour trip, but since I am very much immuno-compromised and cannot travel in a commercial plane and since I need a pressurized cabin for my lungs and since to rent a private plane would cost over $8,000 one way and since I have accumulated quite a few possessions in Philadelphia, we all agree that Daddy will rent a van and drive us home.

And Granny finally takes down the blue ribbon that she tied around the old hickory nut tree, back on November 16, 1994.

One hundred and seventy three days have passed.

Our hearts are overjoyed with gladness.

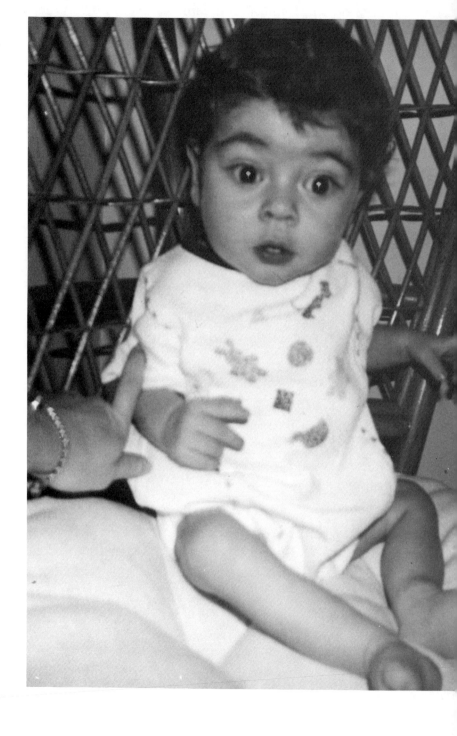

A STEP BACKWARDS

CHAPTER XV

James 1:2-3 (RSV)
"Count it all joy, my brethren, when you meet various trials, for you know that the testing of your faith produces steadfastness."

The first night back home, Mommy puts me in my "gramps cradle." Guess what? I don't have enough room to roll. I've gotten too big! So I go directly into my own room with my own crib. **Yes!**

Mommy spends most of the night cleaning the house. All those weekend trips to Philadelphia kept Daddy too busy to vacuum and dust. I don't think the house plants will be revived no matter how much water Mommy pours on them. And I don't think the fleas from the cats will die without the house being fumigated. Minor problems. But after such an emotional ordeal, they seem more than annoying.

I can tell Mommy and Daddy are exhausted because they argue. They argue about big things, little things, and everything in between. I try not to add any extra stress, but I am without even realizing it.

I have this aversion to anybody putting anything in or near my mouth. I have on occasion taken a bite or two of baby food but mostly medicines are what I take orally. Then there are all the horrible procedures like suctioning and awful tubes like the breathing tube that were hooked up to my ventilator. That's what my mouth is used for, so I'm not too keen on eating. Actually I put up quite a fuss and refuse my bottle. Both Mommy and I hate the NG-tube but the alternative of Mommy spoon feeding me my formula is very time consuming and kinda messy. There's just no good solution.

The doctor flips when she sees our feeding routine and isn't impressed with my meager weight gains, low SATS, and blood work. When I return in twenty-four hours with a fever, I am diagnosed with an ear infection and major dehydration and immediately admitted to MCG.

BUMMER. Freedom lasted for only six short days!

The PICU at MCG hasn't changed much since I've been gone. Same nurses. Same doctors. Even the same room. Any thoughts I had of this being a quick stay are shattered when tests indicate that I have major blood clots in the neck and shoulder area. The blood clots are causing my face to swell and are a result of the dehydration that is a result of the combination of my fever from my ear infection and the continued use of diuretics needed to keep my kidneys functioning. My bodily functions are a finely tuned balance regulated by fifteen medicines. ANYTHING that disrupts the balance causes trouble. I'm in big trouble. Again.

※ ※ ※ ※ ※

It takes over two weeks to dissolve the blood clots. Feels more like two months. To top it off, my chest x-rays are looking hazy now and so the doctors decide to treat me for rejection. Three massive doses of steroids over a three day period and I'm discharged from the hospital.

Just in time for Granny's visit. She still has her favorite camera with her. I'm getting smarter. I close my eyes each time she goes to take my picture and I don't see those silly red dots. Of course my photos all look like I'm asleep. Ha Ha. Fooled you, Granny!

Since I'm still not eating much, Granny spends most of her waking hours coaxing me to attempt to eat. She's also trying to coordinate some kind of home health assistance for Mommy so she can have a little break. Both jobs are proving to be more difficult than Granny anticipated. After five days and partial success, she leaves. Less than twenty-four hours later, I'm rushed back to CHOP on an emergency medi-jet flight. The diagnosis is acute rejection.

Four days of tests help Dr. Bridges determine that I'm not in rejection, and Daddy, Mommy and I return to Augusta on an Angel of Mercy Flight. Granny comes back too. She only stays for three days, but she helps Daddy, Mommy, and me start looking for a house. We're renting now, but we hope to buy our own house so that we can make it more "medically friendly" for my condition. I really handle the search well, considering I'm not much into house hunting.

As my face begins to get puffy again, Mommy becomes alarmed since it reminds her of the symptoms she saw with my blood clots just a month ago. She's right. Another blood clot. I was hoping I would get to stay out of the hospital for an entire month, but it's not going to happen.

One bright spot did occur. We celebrate my month birth-days--which I consider an excellent idea--and for the first time I was home for my "birthday"--my eighth month birthday. This was a huge moment for all of us. An occasion to really party!

Now, however, it's back to MCG. My whole right side is continuing to swell and it is uncomfortable. My ear is five times it's normal size. My eye is swollen shut. My right arm is humongous. When will all this get better?

For four more weeks the doctors continue to treat me. They give me the blood thinner coumadin to the extent that I literally bleed from every God-given hole in my body as well as all the man-made ones. I finally am wheeled to the OR for surgery to establish an arterial line only after seven very long and excruciating hours of probing, pricking, and jabbing, with no sedative or medication to ease the pain.

This is the second time I have endured hours upon hours of

torture trying to locate access to my blood system. I do believe these days are the absolute worst days of my life. Looking at Mommy confirms my belief. My pain is her pain. If there's one consolation--for the doctors, not me--I can't cry loud enough for them to truly know the extent of my agony.

And once again I take a step backwards. I am flown via medi-jet back to Philadelphia.

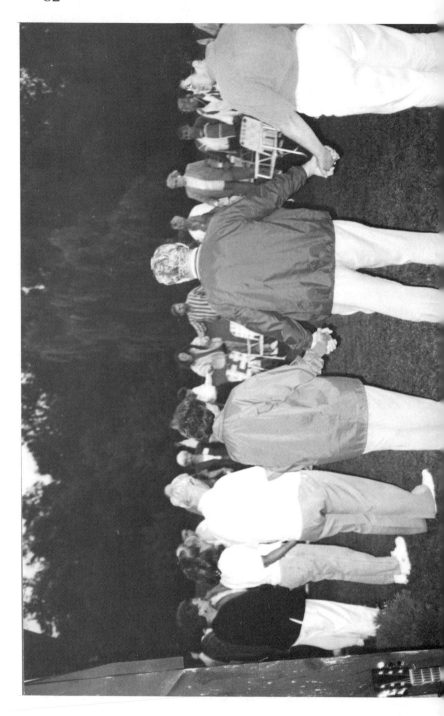

PRAYER CHAINS AROUND THE WORLD

CHAPTER XVI

James 5:13-16 (RSV)
"Is any among you suffering? Let him pray. Is any cheer-ful? Let him sing praise. Is any among you sick? Let him call for the elders of the church and let them pray over him, anointing him with oil in the name of the Lord; and the prayer of faith will save the sick man and the Lord will raise him up. . . ."

During this roller coaster ride with all its ups and downs, my entire family is steadfastly continuing to pray. From day one when Granny called her church and other churches and friends and prayer chains in her community they have been faithful in their prayers. Great-grandma Jean also has her church and friends praying for me as well as Grandma Kay's and Grandpa George's church. Uncle Randy's seminary, and Aunt Lynn's church. Aunt Sandi even has requested prayer from friends like Kevin Johnson and David Robinson of the NBA. I know both my Uncle Hosses and Aunt Tammi hold me up in prayer. I am surrounded by prayer.

One day Granny brings me a pile of letters and shows me my name. That's all that looks familiar in most of the letters be-cause they are not written in English. They are written in Por-tuguese and in Spanish because they come from wonderful people in Brazil and Cuba. People who have never seen me, yet who are praying daily for my health and for Mommy and Daddy's strength, and even for my extended family.

I know Geráld, Granny's taxi driver friend, prays for me daily Eric Colemen, the outgoing Christian man who cleans my hos pital room here in Philadelphia, prays for me. He's even laid hands on me for healing.

The Billy Graham prayer team, the Norman Vincent Peale Center, the Cove, the Jews for Jesus, Dr. Dobson, Dave Draveky's Outreach of Hope, Gateway to Joy, Back to the Bible and the Upper Room are some of the ministries who pray for me.

My great-aunt Karen in Florida prays for me. My great-uncle Doug and his family in California pray for me. Mommy re ceives a letter from a man in Uganda who is praying for me Missionaries in Africa are praying for me.

"Please Pray for Joshua" signs go up in Mercer and in the local newspaper's classified ads.

Prayer is powerful. Prayer is real. Prayer keeps us strong Even now when I'm hospitalized for the fourth time in as many months, prayer gives us peace.

Mommy finds comfort when she's praying, knowing God is in control. She says she is learning to accept the circumstances we find ourselves in and to be content. I realize that in so doing the pain does not go away, it merely becomes bearable. I try to be like Mommy. We both still cry every day, but we also con tinue to trust God. Completely.

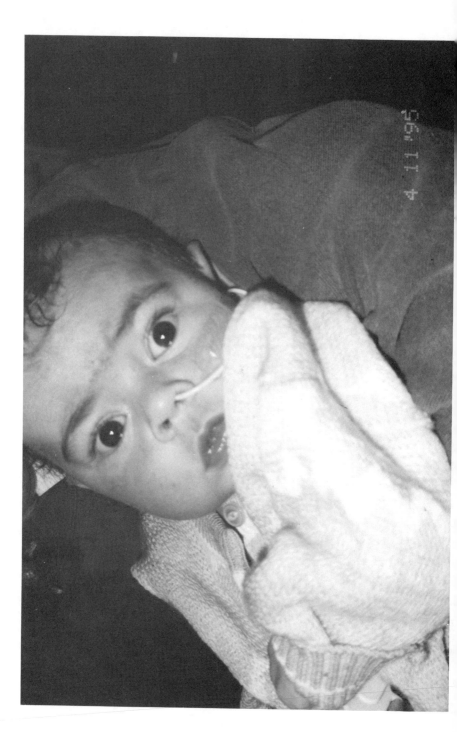

MILLION DOLLAR BABY

CHAPTER XVII

II Corinthians 8:9 (KJV)
"For ye know the grace of our Lord Jesus Christ, that, though
e was rich, yet for your sakes he became poor, that ye through
is poverty might be rich."

As long as I'm in the hospital for the blood clots, Dr. Bridges
1inks it might be a good idea to put a tube directly into my
1mmy to feed me and to give me my medicine. They call it a G-
1be. The good thing about a G-tube is that I won't have to take
fteen medicines (some more than once) daily by mouth. Of
ourse I will continue taking the absolute worst tasting one--
yclosporine--by mouth because the medicine is oil-based and
vill stick to my plastic tubing. It is imperative I receive the
bsolute correct dosage to keep my body from rejecting my new
ungs. The second good thing will be Mommy can stop spoon
eeding me my formula. I know she hates having the G-tube
ut in my stomach as much as I dislike it, but we both agree it
eats sticking the NG-tube down my nose for every feeding. I
uppose if I would leave the tube alone between feedings the
roblem would be solved. However, it is so annoying I can't
keep from yanking it out.

So seven months to the day after my transplant, I go into
urgery again. When I come out, I have my new G-tube. To
prevent me from being even tempted to tug on it, I'm immediately dressed in a one piece outfit. I'm pretty sharp looking, if I

do say so myself.

The doctors also take this opportunity to put a portacath under my skin in my right chest area. No more seven hour probes to find a line.

With all the downsizing at SRS, Daddy needs to get back to work. So we drive home again instead of waiting for the Angel of Mercy flight. We definitely want Daddy's employer to stay satisfied with him because most of my medical expenses are paid by Daddy's insurance.

I was originally on Mommy's insurance policy until she had to quit her job. Now I've been transferred to Daddy's. Occasionally the bills are still misfiled under Mommy's forms and then the hospitals get all upset that payment won't be made. They really panic. Of course I have quite a healthy bill.

God certainly is providing for my medical expenses. Way back in January when Dr. Steinhart went directly to option number four, Mommy and Daddy were contacted by the social worker explaining ways to raise enough money to partially afford my transplant. Benefits. She called them fund-raising benefits.

Mommy and Daddy were already stressed to the maximum. Where did the social worker expect them to find the time and energy for raising money?

God provided. He provided DeDe Hicks and Marc Waltz. They had a chicken roast for me. Five hundred chickens. Bought, cooked, and sold. They also had a golf scramble with all proceeds going to my transplant fund.

God provided the Billie Belding family. In their time of grief when Billie's wife Barbara died, it was their wish that all material contributions be donated to my transplant fund. I am still very moved by their thoughtfulness.

God provided Trinity Presbyterian Church in Mercer. They had a fund-raising luncheon as well as encouraged Rev. Crooks to bring the generous check from the adult Sunday School class to Philadelphia.

God provided the Suffern, New York Presbyterian Church.

That's my Great-grandma Jean's church. They donated to my trust fund.

God provided Diana Jackal, the mother of one of Mommy's high school classmates, who put jars in many of the local businesses in Mercer as well as a "Wishing Well" for donations.

God provided the YMCA where Mommy teaches aerobics. They set up a trust fund.

God provided the First Western Bank in Mercer County which also established a trust fund.

God provided Roberto Bermudez Rosette, a young Cuban artist, who, in his desire to be of service to God and to help me, has sent several prints from his native land to Granny to sell. All proceeds will go directly into my trust fund.

God continues to provide individuals who generously donate to these funds.

No one has actually added up my entire debit side of my ledger, but here are a few interesting statistics:

A hospital room in CICU in CHOP costs $3,000.00 per day.

My monthly medicine and nutrition costs are well over $1,500.00, and when I'm put on a food substitute, the cost jumps to $7,500.00 per month.

MCG charges $800.00 per day for the hospital bed. A separate charge is incurred to use any item in the room. A sticker is put on each patient's charge sheet daily when something is used. My sheets have stickers ON stickers.

$300,000.00 for a "no-frills" lung transplant. Add to that the operating room, anesthesiologist, radiologist, etc.

My ten minute biopsies cost $15,000.00 each.

My plan is to stay out of the hospital from now on so that I won't add any more expenses to my already seven figure debt. Unfortunately, my plan fails when I'm readmitted to MCG just five days after I leave CHOP for the third time. This time I'm having severe breathing problems. More tests. More transfusions. More x-rays. More, more, more. I'm getting so weary. Everyone is getting weary. Life continues to be on hold.

I'm really happy to go home after nine days in the hospital and don't even mind returning daily as an outpatient for x-rays and a barium swallow (checking for reflux). Granny comes to stay with Mommy and me while Daddy goes on a business trip. She's a big help carrying my oxygen tank and baby bag while Mommy carries me. We're very careful to keep me covered with a blanket while we're in the hospital so I don't catch any "bugs." It's cold and flu season and we have to be very cautious--especially in the hospital.

❋ ❋ ❋ ❋ ❋

I'm having trouble keeping my formula down, and Dr. Valera Hudson, my pulmonologist, thinks I'd better come in to be safe. Earlier this morning I threw up the funniest looking "thing." Mommy kids that it's part of my new lung, but both she and Granny instinctively know something is definitely amiss. She conscientiously saves it in a plastic bag and brings it in to show Dr. Hudson.

My visit takes longer than any of us expected. We're all visibly upset when Dr. Hudson insists that I once again be hospitalized. My "lung thing" is actually tissue called a cast. Something rare and indicative of a severe lymphatic problem. Her concern is very apparent.

I think Granny takes it the hardest. She tries to be brave for Mommy and me, but it's a losing battle. She cries uncontrollably. She cries so much she can't see because her contacts get all fogged up.

I'm not in the PICU this time, so Mommy and Granny plan to stay with me in my new room. Granny leaves to call several of our faithful prayer partners and tearfully explains that once again I'm doing poorly. They pray together. They cry together. Granny feels better. We sleep well.

In the morning, Dr. Hudson cancels her plans to go out of town so she can be near me if there's a problem--but--SURPRISE!! I'm fine. Really fine. Dr. Hudson's pleased. Mommy's overjoyed. I'm ecstatic. Dr. Hudson admits that there is no medical explanation for such a turn around. We thank God.

I'm not just a million dollar baby in the financial sense, but also in the spiritual sense: God continues to invest in me daily.

TURNING ONE

CHAPTER XVIII

II Peter 3:18 (NIV)
"But grow in the grace and knowledge of our Lord and Savior Jesus Christ. To Him be glory both now and forever. Amen."

Before I'm discharged from MCG (for the fifth time), Dr. Hudson and her partner Dr. Margaret Guill decide to try to prevent any more casts by putting me on a food substitute called hyperale. Sounds fine. Where's the door? Mommy and I want to go home. Daddy's back. Granny's left and we want to celebrate my eleven month birthday out of the hospital.

We do!

I have one good week.

I have two good weeks.

I have three good weeks.

I have four good weeks. I set a record. No hospitalizations. No major problems. My twelve month birthday is coming. I'm going to celebrate my real FIRST birthday. At home. With Granny, Grandma Kay, and Grandpa George. After we're done celebrating (no candle because of my oxygen), we're gonna move into our new house. Give my Mommy and Daddy four good weeks and they can accomplish more than most people can in four months.

Just for Granny I really "ham it up" for her ritual photo shoot. After all it's my real birthday. I don't shut my eyes even once. I smile occasionally, but even when I'm not down right smiling I give a nice, pleasant look. I like my toys. I like my company. I like my party, but I don't like my cake. I still have this thing about food and swallowing and that kind of thing. So I "pass" on the refreshments. All in all it's a wonderful time.

✻ ✻ ✻ ✻ ✻

I can't help but reflect on my donor's family. We all do that. More than anyone realizes.

✻ ✻ ✻ ✻ ✻

Granny and Mommy hurry over to our new house to paint my room blue and to hang a beautiful rainbow border at the ceiling. Then they hurry back to begin packing. Within twenty-four hours, with the help of Daddy's whole family and a few good friends, we are officially moved into our new house. It's really great--all on one floor--and we even have a big back yard with a swimming pool for my physical therapy. Chelsie and Tasha aren't too sure they belong here but they'll adjust. If I can adjust to breathing on oxygen and being fed through a tube, and if Daddy and Mommy can adjust to no sleep and no free time, I know the cats can adjust to living outside our beautiful new home.

I'm thankful to be one year old.

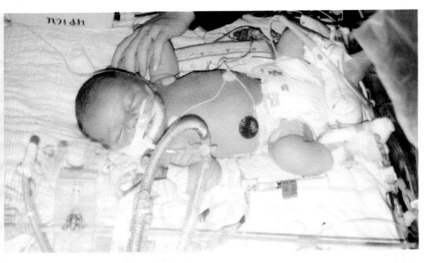

Baby Joshua

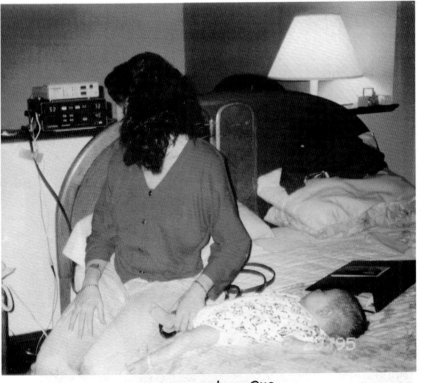

Are my numbers OK?

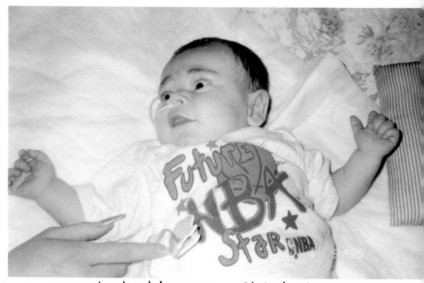

Look out, here comes Air Joshua!

Any germs around?

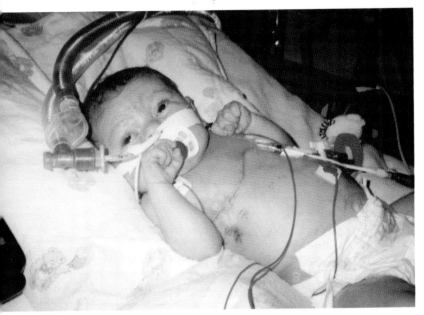

Woe is me!

Oh no, Granny's taking another picture!

I love you, Mommy.

Daddy, please can I borrow the car?

Thank you, God

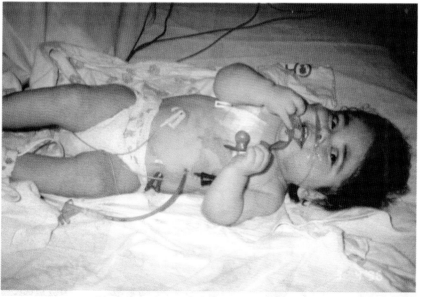

Check out my G-tube & portacath

If I stand on my tip toes I'm taller than my oxygen tank.

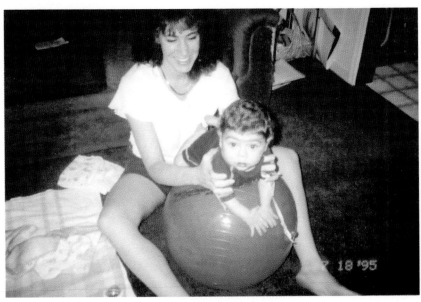

"Let's Get Physical"

Merry Christmas!

Birthday parties are fun!

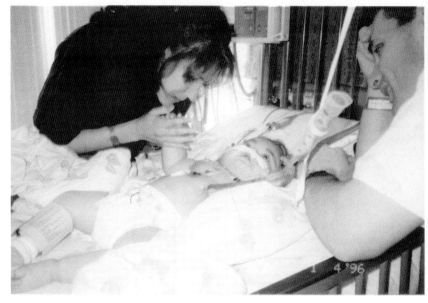

A rough night.

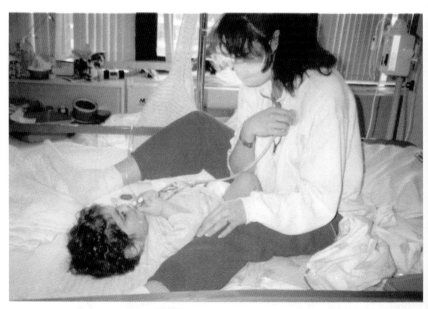

Your heart sounds fine, mommy.

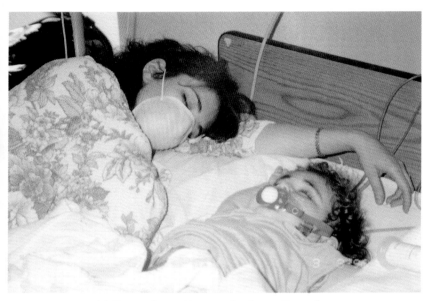

At the exhaustive end of another day.

Who ate my donut?

Am I cool or what?

Monkey see
Monkey do

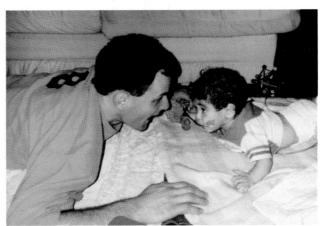

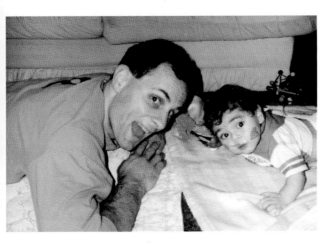

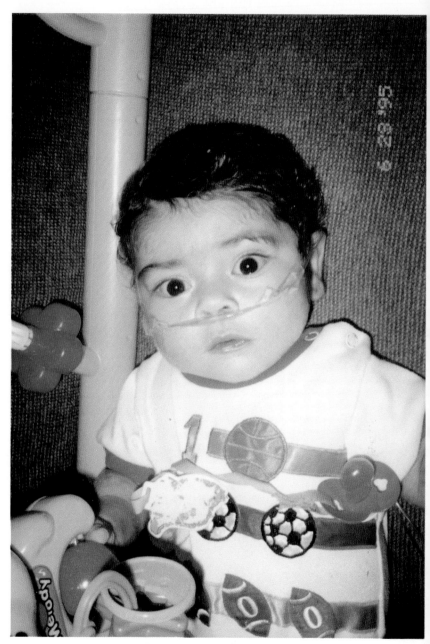

Bright eyes

BAPTISM
CHAPTER XIX

Mark 16:16 (KJV)
"He that believeth and is baptized shall be saved; but he that believeth not shall be damned."

This is my first trip to Lakemont Presbyterian Church. I know they've been praying for me. I know they know I'm coming. Everyone has been warned of my fragile condition and precautions have been taken to keep me from coming in contact with any germs.

Mommy, Granny, and I wait in Pastor Jack Jagoditsch's study. The Sunday church hour begins. Daddy sits in the congregation with Grandpa George, Grandma Kay, Aunt Lynn, Uncle John, and Daniel. He comes and gets us. Mommy carries me. Granny carries the oxygen tank. We come in through a side door which brings us almost directly to the alter. I've never been anywhere with this many people before.

The usual custom in infant baptism is for the minister to hold the baby. In my case, Mommy continues to hold me, with Daddy standing close by. Pastor Jack dips his fingers in the Baptismal water and places them on my head. He baptizes me "in the name of the Father, Son, and Holy Ghost." His words are genuine and comforting. He explains that this is a symbol of salvation and that it is Daddy's and Mommy's way of professing their faith in Jesus Christ as Savior, that it is their desire that I also know Him as my Savior and that they dedicate my life to Him.

Then Mommy thanks the congregation for their overwhelm
ing support and concern. They have been so faithful in their
prayers. They have truly ministered to us by bringing food and
flowers and donating money to my trust fund. Their acts of
kindness have been a blessing beyond words.

Mommy holds me tight. Her tears roll down her cheeks and
I feel them, warm and wet through my beautiful white jump suit
bought especially for this occasion. I feel her heart beat.
know this is a very special moment in our lives. Mommy and
Daddy are publicly dedicating me to the Lord who has guided
my life from birth. To the God who has protected me, blessed
me, and loved me beyond anything I could imagine. To the King
of Kings, Prince of Peace. To Jesus Christ who is my personal
Savior.

This congregation has the privilege of hearing publicly what
privately I've known forever. I want the whole world to know.
belong to Jesus. Yesterday, today, and tomorrow.

Jesus Saves.

Praise God. I am His.

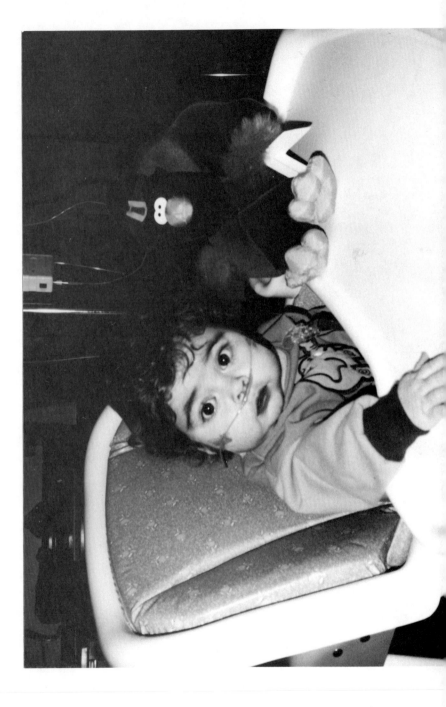

DR. SPRAY'S REUNION

CHAPTER XX

Romans 8:28 (RSV)
"And we know in all things God works for the good of those
who love him, who have been called according to his pur-
pose."

The remainder of November is actually quite uneventful.
Mommy, Daddy, and I have a quiet Thanksgiving dinner in our
new home. I have my good days and not so good days, but all in
all the urgency of life and death matters seems to be over.

We arrange for the Shriners to fly me up to Philadelphia.
The plan is for me to have possible surgery to reroute my lymph
system and to stay long enough to attend a party that Dr. Spray
is hosting for all the lung transplant patients. The party sounds
good, but the surgery seems too radical.

Lisa was the first lung transplant at CHOP. She's nineteen
years old. I was the second and the youngest. Then came Ronak
who is two years old and Shyla who is twelve. I was still recuperating when they got their lungs. After I left, Lexie (two and
one half), Molly (five), and Vanessa (two) received their lungs.
Molly actually received a heart and lungs. Then Spencer (five)
and Amy, who to date was last. Everyone has returned except
Amy. She doesn't live in the continental United States. (I forget
where she lives.) But we all are part of Dr. Spray's family and
so we all are family to each other. A common bond unites us.

The day of the party is cold and snowy. How come I keep

coming north in the winter? Mommy tells me that she much prefers Georgia weather, especially December through March.

I'm not feeling well today. I'm beginning to swell again, and if Dr. Spray wasn't so special to me, I think I might be tempted to skip the party. Mommy tells me we won't stay long. It's not like we have to travel far. It's being held right here in another wing of the hospital.

We go but I can't quite bring myself to have fun. I meet Lexie for the first time. She isn't feeling well either. Her Mommy says Lexie will be my girlfriend when I get older. I think I like that. She's very pretty. She doesn't have a voice either, only she's learning sign language. I wish I knew how to sign, "Hello."

I also see Spencer's Mommy. She's a graduate of Bucknell University in Lewisburg, PA. The same college my Mommy graduated from. What a small world. We became friends back in April while Spencer was waiting for his transplant and we were living at the Ronald McDonald House.

I wish I was feeling better.

I continue to feel lousy after the party. The doctors decide to postpone my surgery. Granny comes and goes on a quick visit to celebrate Mommy's birthday. Aunt Sandi and Uncle Ronnie also come for short "pick me up" visits. We appreciate the company. It's difficult spending another pre-holiday season in the hospital.

Everyone is amazed that I'm getting fatter. It's about time I put some weight on my skinny legs. The hyperale is doing its job. But it's also beginning to destroy my liver. Soon another feeding change will be needed.

Without warning, we are given permission to leave as soon as we can find a pressurized jet to fly me home. The Angel Flight only has one such plane and it's in for repairs. Everyone makes calls, but it's so close to Christmas we aren't having any luck. Just when we're almost ready to rent a plane, Westinghouse offers their corporate jet.

Daddy, Mommy, and I are headed south.

HOME FOR THE HOLIDAYS
CHAPTER XXI

I Corinthians 2:9 (NIV)
"However as it is written: No eye has seen, no ear has heard, no mind has conceived what God has prepared for those who love him."

My first Christmas--home, that is.

We have the tree, the lights, the presents. We even have the true meaning--the birth of our Lord, baby Jesus--but we are missing something. ME. I'm really sick. My face and upper body continue to get more and more swollen. I moan the best I'm able in order to let Mommy and Daddy know my condition.

The doctors are aware of my plight. To save my liver they have taken me off the hyperale. We are going to have to "tough this one out." The thought actually comes to mind that maybe I'm home to die. Maybe the doctors want us to have the memory of one special holiday home together. If so, this is going to be a rough memory. Each day that passes I get worse.

My constant suffering and pain casts a dark shadow over all the normally bright lights of Christmas. It's almost like the shadow of the cross falling upon the manger. Perhaps God is giving me a glimpse of how He understands Christmas.

Perhaps He is blessing me more than any tinsel-type holiday could.

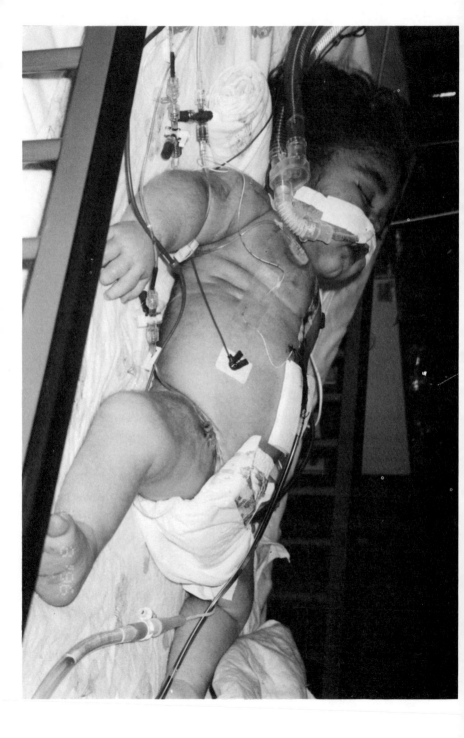

FOCUS ON THE LORD
CHAPTER XXII

Hebrews 12:2 (NIV)
"Let us fix our eyes on Jesus, the author and perfecter of our faith, who for the joy set before him endured the cross, scorning its shame. . . ."

December 29, 1995 finds me back in the hospital at MCG. December 31, 1995 finds Dr. Pearson-Shaver once again flying up to Philadelphia with Daddy, Mommy, and me. I'm in pretty bad shape.

I certainly don't mind saying goodbye to 1995. I spent two hundred and seventy one days of the year in the hospital. **Please God, let 1996 be healthier.**

Granny flies to Philadelphia on January 2. She arrives too late to see me before I'm taken for my heart catheterization. I've had one catheterization back when I was just a little baby in Georgia, but it didn't go well. So everyone's a little apprehensive about this one.

Granny's journal reads, *"Flew to Philadelphia. Was twenty minutes late arriving because plane had to be de-iced. Went directly to CHOP. Joshua already getting catheterization. After about a half hour a nurse comes and asks us to go to the 4th floor to see Dr. Bridges. Dr. Bridges explains that there is good news and bad news. The good news: hopefully, finally, they found Joshua's problem. A blocked vein--superior vena cava (SVC). The bad news: while repairing the SVC, the stent (a piece of metal wire mesh used to open up blocked blood vessels) acciden-*

tally fell into Joshua's heart. He will need immediate open heart surgery to retrieve it. Human error. Instinctively I start calling prayer chains. On the flight to Philly I had much time to reflect on God's grace and mercies. He has brought us through the valley of shadow of death before. And He will again."

I'm completely sedated when the nurses wheel me to Mommy, Daddy, and Granny. We take the back elevator and can only stay for a minute. I have to be prepped for my surgery. Everyone cries. I know I look bad. The nurses remind them that I can hear. Even though I look like I'm in a coma, I'm actually just paralyzed. Mommy holds my hand and tells me how much she loves me. Daddy gives me words of encouragement. Granny sings, "Jesus Loves Me." That's my favorite song. So many times when things were looking bad or I was in pain or discouraged Granny sang "Jesus Loves Me" or played it on my tape recorder.

That's all the time we have together. I'm gone before I get to say goodbye.

I know Granny is pondering Aunt Tammi's words about how baby's have heart surgery. I will be packed in ice to bring my body temperature down. Then my heart is stopped, repaired, and restarted. It can take no longer than twenty minutes. I'm sure Mommy and Daddy are pondering the words Dr. Bridges has just uttered. She reassured them that Dr. Spray can fix anything. He'll do the surgery. It will be a little more difficult because of the scar tissue from the transplant. But, Dr. Spray will fix it.

I once again ponder Granny's words, "God will not take Joshua Home."

And now is the best time of all to focus not on the mistakes but on the Lord. To remember that God is Omnipotent. He directs our paths. He holds us in the palm of His hand. He breathes life into us. Without Him we are nothing. He is in charge. We must trust and obey Him.

✳ ✳ ✳ ✳ ✳

After what seems to be an eternity, Mommy, Daddy, Granny, and I are reunited in my room in the CICU.

THE BLIZZARD OF '96

CHAPTER XXIII

II Corinthians 5:7 (KJV)
"For we walk by faith, not by sight."

My recovery seems so slow. I'm once again back on the ventilator and I have lines going everywhere.

My prognosis seems to be good. Dr. Bridges and Dr. Spray seem to think that the SVC has been my problem for a good part of the time. If I understand this right, as long as I was fed the I.V. hyperale, my nourishment went directly into my blood stream below the constricted "problem area" and didn't cause any backup of fluids in my upper body, so my swelling would improve. However, when I was fed through my G-tube, all the fluids had to go through the constricted vein and got backed up which caused my entire upper body to swell like a balloon. I'm so glad that the planned surgery last month was postponed. Had the doctors rerouted my lymph system I would be in a terrible mess. The surgery was irreversible. Now we can see it was also unnecessary.

It's a good thing that I'm off the hyperale. It kept me nutritionally sound, but it also was destroying my liver. The doctors continue to monitor my liver function to be certain no permanent damage occurred.

For the last few hospital stays one family member has been spending all night with me. It began because Mommy brings my medicines from home to help save the insurance company unnecessary medical costs. She also administers all medications that I normally get during each twenty-four hour period. (The nurses are in charge of any new medicines pertaining to the hospital stay.) In order to give my medicines, Mommy, Daddy, or Granny sleeps in the room with me.

Tonight it is Daddy's turn. He's going to fly back home tomorrow and work all week and return on the weekend. You know--that alternating thing with Granny. But when we wake up and look out the window all we can see is WHITE. It snowed. Actually it more than snowed. It "blizzarded." Thirty inches!

Daddy thinks it's great. The airport is closed. The roads are all closed. The entire city of Philadelphia is closed. The National Guard is called upon to bring in the nurses and doctors. Emergency Snow Removal is in effect and no one is allowed on the roads. Mommy and Granny have a real problem getting to the hospital from the RMH. But Daddy--a true Southerner--goes out and catches snowflakes on his tongue.

The nurses do double and triple shifts. This is a bad time to be having all the problems I'm having. My heart rate is elevated. I have thick yellow secretions. I once again test positive for serratia (a bacteria common among ventilated patients).

The Governor of Pennsylvania declares Philadelphia a disaster area. I wonder if Dr. Spray would consider declaring me a disaster area?

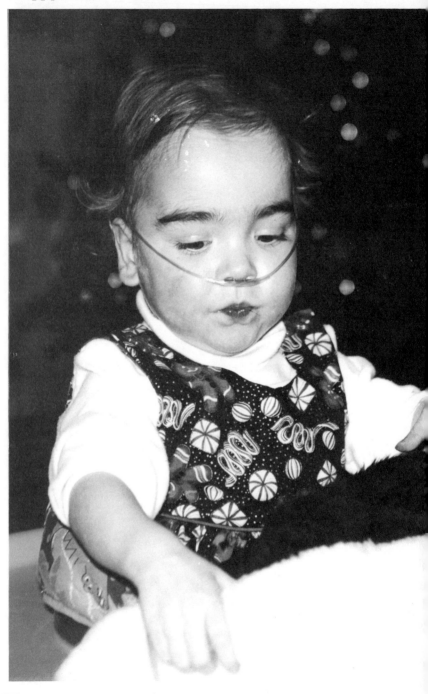

LEXIE

CHAPTER XXIV

Mark 10:14 (KJV)
*". . . suffer the little children to come unto me and forbid
hem not: for of such is the kingdom of God."*

My girlfriend, Lexie, is in the hospital room next to mine. We
have a common wall between our rooms with a window. Even
hough we can look back and forth when the curtain isn't drawn
closed, we seldom do. She's even sicker than I am.

Eight days have come and gone since my open heart surgery.
Time to be extubated. AGAIN. I'm an "old hat" at this. I know
Mommy will hold her breath until my breathing is normal, but
his time I am sure I will have no problems at all. There has
been quite a debate over "should we" or "shouldn't we." I'm
continuing to have these thick yellow secretions. No one can
explain why.

The "should we's" win. I'm fine. Twenty minutes pass.
Mommy holds me. Daddy holds me. We play. Then out of the
blue I go into respiratory arrest. I stop breathing. My body
stiffens. I turn gray and my heart rate drops to thirty. Granny
drops to her knees in prayer. Daddy gives me emergency oxygen and Mommy runs to the nurses' station for help.

Dr. Lenny reintubates me through my mouth which is the
quickest and easiest way to get my lungs working again. There
are nurses and doctors all around my bed. Just like a scene
from the TV show, <u>ER</u>. But the crisis is over. God has once

again protected me in my time of need.

In order to clear up the secretions, Dr. Bridges gives me th same medicine cystic fibrosis lungs receive.

While I go through these difficult times, Lexie goes throug even worse. She's rejecting her lungs and needs another trans plant. Earlier, Vanessa had to be retransplanted. Her secon set is working fine.

We all pray for Lexie. We all pray for each other.

Lexie reminds Mommy and Daddy of me more than any c the other transplant patients. Her eyes "float" occasionally lik mine. Her voice is almost non-existent like mine. She's sma for her age like I am. She sucks her pacifier (binky) by usin the back of her hand just like I do. We're soul mates.

Lexie has been medically paralyzed ever since we came bac to CHOP on New Year's Eve. Her condition continues to ge more grave. She's kept alive by a big machine.

Then we hear the helicopter landing and Lexie's Mom knock on the window and lets us know that Lexie has her second se of lungs on the way. We all rejoice. Dr. Spray's gonna fix Lexie

My recovery begins to quicken. I once again am extubatec My lungs work fine this time. I actually eat a little solid food.

I'm feeling much better. I hope Lexie's feeling better too.

It's time for me to be discharged. Our plane is fogged ir That gives Mommy time to say goodbye to Lexie's family. She still having a rough time.

We leave.

Two days later the call comes that Lexie has died.

We all cry lots.

I've lost my first girlfriend, but I know I've gained a Guardia Angel.

Say hi to Jesus for me, Lexie.

In Memory Of "Lexie"

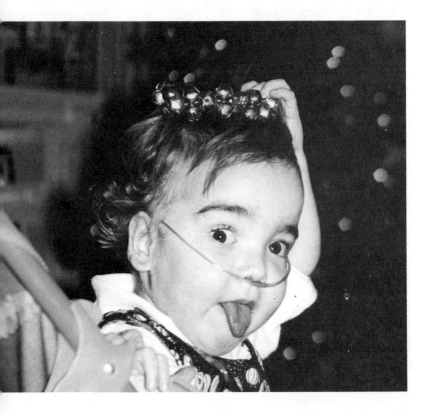

Cameron Alexis White
5/31/93-1/19/96

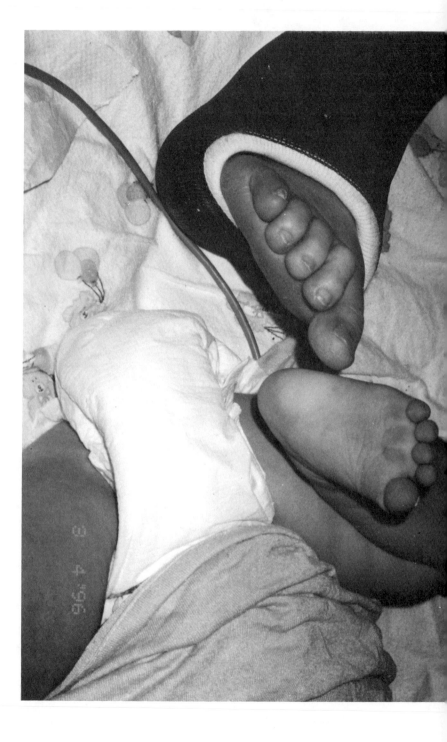

ANOTHER CRISIS
CHAPTER XXV

Isaiah 57:19 (NIV)
"Peace, peace to those far and near, says the Lord. And I will heal them."

I'm so excited. Granny and Gramps are driving down from Mercer to see me. The weather here is so much nicer than Pennsylvania's. I'm feeling much better. I still need oxygen to breathe and I still take all my medicines and food through my G-tube. But no big deal.

We enjoy the short three days together. We take walks and rides in the car and Gramps sits in the car with me while Mommy and Granny run errands. I kinda test Gramps' babysitting ability. I cry to see what he does. He flunks the test. As soon as Mommy comes into view I quiet down. Gramps is going to have to work on his grandfatherly duties. But we do one fun thing together. Mommy cuts my hair for the first time while Granny cuts Gramps' hair. We sit side by side and neither one of us cries. We bond.

✳ ✳ ✳ ✳ ✳

I have my ups.

I have my downs.

I like my ups better. But I don't like "up-chucking." And that's what both Mommy and I are doing today. Mommy's really worried that we caught something from her friend's daughter. She asks Daddy to call the friend because three days ago they stopped by for a visit and one of her daughters showed signs of being sick. Sure enough. The phone call confirms Mommy's fear: the FLU.

My fever is over 103 degrees Farenheit. This brings back awful memories of how the ear infection caused the delicate balance of medicines to go hay-wire and landed me in the hospital for over a month.

Don't look now, but it IS happening AGAIN. First we go to the emergency room. I'm quickly admitted to the PICU. The culture grows something overnight. The blood work indicates an infection. I have a blood clot in my subclavian and I'm in respiratory distress. All this from what the public would consider the average twenty-four hour flu.

There are two different ways for treating me this time. The Georgia doctors have one way. The Philadelphia doctors have another way. Since I'm in Georgia, we're doing it the Georgia doctors' way. I'm given massive doses of a potent antibiotic. I'm put in an oxygen tent. Things seem to be getting better when a nurse accidently spills water into my oxygen tube. I, of course, breathe it and have a terrible reaction. This has a damaging effect on my recovery and so Mommy, Daddy, and I join the frequent flyer group again and return to Pennsylvania. If I weren't so sick, I might wonder how many miles we have flown.

Daddy needs to return to work so Mommy calls Granny. Of course she comes--crutches and all. Last week Granny broke her ankle. She looks funny with her camera AND her crutches! For six long days she hobbles to and fro trying to help.

During this time, the doctors are planning to take the portacath out of my heart. It's pretty certain that the plastic tubing in the portacath has become infected and is putting me at a very high risk for a heart infection (since the portacath tip lies directly in my heart.) But as always I'm not the normal case. There is much discussion as to the benefits and liabilities of keeping this foreign object in my body. During the debate I continue to improve and so the final decision is: the portacath stays and I leave.

Back to Georgia.

Another crisis is history.

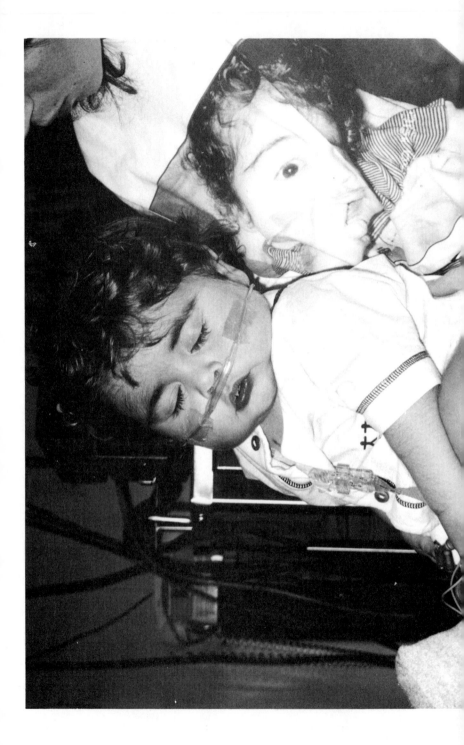

JESUS LOVES ME THIS I KNOW
CHAPTER XXVI

I Corinthians 13:7-8 (RSV)
"Love bears all things, believes all things, hopes all things, endures all things. Love never ends. . . ."

Over the last eighteen months the doctors have prepared Mommy and Daddy for my death several times. Each time we requested countless prayers. Granny says she's read magazine articles stating that studies have been done proving prayer works. Not that we need some dumb magazine article to tell us THAT. We know from experience. We have a list longer than my G-tube. I'll share it with you.

1.   They prayed that I might live and that my heart would be repaired. And it was. Thank You, Lord Jesus.

2.   They prayed that as I spent days, weeks, and months in the ICU in the hospital that I would be protected from the many persistent and often life threatening viruses. God heard and was merciful.

3.   They prayed that the experimental drug--nitric oxide-- would be safe and continue to work during my flight to Philadelphia. I was the first person from MCG ever to fly while being kept alive with nitric oxide. God's hand remained on me and all went well.

4.   They prayed that I, after being diagnosed with a hypoplastic heart, would not need the three surgeries necessary for survival. The next day the doctors reversed their diagnosis.

124

Thank You, Lord Jesus.

5.   They prayed that I would receive new lungs before my old ones gave out. Within twenty-four hours of being listed as a recipient, I was in surgery. Halleluia! Praise God! Thank You, Lord Jesus.

6.   They prayed that I would be taken off the ventilator. God taught us patience on this one, but Praise His Holy Name. The ventilator is now a memory.

7.   They prayed during my two heart catheterizations. Both were difficult and dangerous because of my size. God heard and was merciful.

8.   They prayed as day after day my tiny blood vessels gave out as a result of the pressure caused by the needles. Deeper and deeper veins needed to be tapped. Twice it took seven hours of picking and probing before surgery was performed. God sustained us. A line was always found.

9.   They prayed for the security of my Daddy's job as he faced two periods of layoffs. His insurance policy has effectively covered the majority of my $2 million plus medical bills. Daddy's layoff would be disastrous. Praise God. Daddy's still employed.

10.   They prayed that I would not become permanently addicted to the massive doses of morphine I was on. Thank You, Lord Jesus.

11.   They prayed for safe trips and good weather for the many air flights. Thank You, Lord Jesus.

12.   They prayed that I would live through a life threatening virus I caught--the rotavirus. Thank You, Lord Jesus.

13.   They prayed I would get off the NG-tube. Thank You, Lord Jesus.

14.   They prayed my kidneys would continue to work. Thank You, Lord Jesus.

15.   They prayed I would learn to suck by mouth. I will take water from a bottle and have shown them I can even eat (by occasionally taking a few bites). Praise God for my progress.

16.   They prayed that my blood clots would be dissolved before entering my heart or lungs. God heard and was merciful.

17.   They prayed I would not have internal bleeding caused by the massive doses of coumadin I needed for the blood clots. God heard and was merciful.

18.   They prayed for success when the doctors performed open heart surgery to retrieve a piece of metal that was accidentally dropped into my heart. God heard and was merciful.

19.   They prayed my liver was not destroyed by using an I.V. liquid food substitute called hyperale. God heard and was merciful.

20.   They prayed that my lymph system would not need radical surgery. Praise God for His steadfast love.

21.   They prayed I would be able to keep my food down and that my constant vomiting from reflux would end. Praise God for His steadfast love.

22.   They prayed that I would grow and gain weight. I'm now 30 pounds and 31 1/2 inches tall. Praise God for His steadfast love.

23.   They prayed I would not be blind. Praise God I see.

24.   They prayed I would not be deaf. Praise God I hear.

25.   They prayed I would have normal neurological responses. Praise God I can sit and I attempt to roll and crawl.

26.   They prayed I would not be mentally deficient. Praise God that I am alert and smart.

27.   They prayed I would get a voice. Praise God I can make noises and say Ma-ma and Da-da.

28.   They prayed my heart would not become infected by the portacath which remains there even today for the doctors to keep access to my blood system. Thank You, Lord Jesus.

29.   They prayed my biopsies (four to date) would show no sign of rejecting my lungs. Thank You, Lord Jesus.

30.   They prayed I would not need surgery to do my last biopsy. Thank You, Lord Jesus.

31.   Last week, they prayed I would recuperate from a cold.

Within twenty-four hours I was markedly better. With my immune system suppressed by drugs, we know God intervened. Thank You, Lord Jesus.

To realize how good God is to me is such a humbling experience. I want to bow on my knees and cry HOLY. (That's the name of a great song, too.) And I will. As soon as I learn to get on my knees. Until then, I will remember each day how much Jesus loves me and how much I love Him.

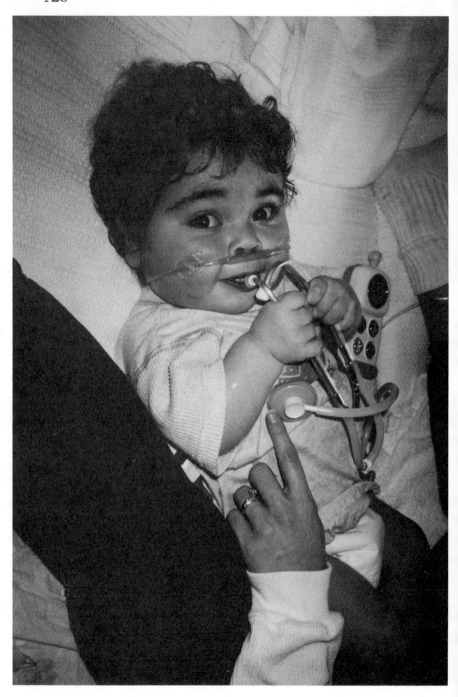

ONWARD CHRISTIAN SOLDIERS

CHAPTER XXVII

John 14:27 (RSV)
"Jesus said, 'Peace I leave with you, my peace I give to you; not as the world gives do I give to you. Let not your heart be troubled, neither let it be afraid.'"

Except for one trip back to Philadelphia for a biopsy and to have my G-tube made into a cute little G-button, I have not returned to the hospital since March 5, 1996. Praise God.

While in Philadelphia, I had the pleasure of seeing the tree that was dedicated in my honor at the completed addition of the Ronald McDonald House. Someday I plan on being well enough to climb that tree--just so Granny can take my picture in it.

I still continue to baffle everyone by refusing any food by mouth. I drink water from a bottle so the experts know I can suck and swallow. I have sixteen teeth so it's not my lack of chewing ability. I'm being given all sorts of new therapies to desensitize me around my mouth and elsewhere, but so far no results.

Since I'm learning sign language, and I'm also starting to become vocal, (I say Ma-ma and Da-da) <u>maybe</u> I'll TELL everyone why I don't eat. Or maybe I'll just start to eat some day.

I continue to need a constant oxygen supply. This also has the doctors confused. The latest thought concerning my inability to breathe without oxygen is that my new lungs became dam-

aged during the problems with my constricted SVC. The hop
is that when I grow my lungs will also grow. Since lung trans
plantation in infants is so new, there is no data to support thi
assumption. But if my lungs do grow, possibly I will outgro\
the damage done. I know that is my prayer.

Probable eye surgery looms in the future. And, of course
with my compromised immune system and countless medica
tions, the possibility of complications from even a common col\
is always a threat. My heart seems healthy. It is neither troublec
nor is it afraid. As always, your prayers are requested. And a
always, I am very grateful.

You might say the medical profession did wonders to sav
my life. You might say I've had a life changing experience o
actually more than one. You might say I'm a pretty lucky littl
boy. YOU might say that. Not me.

I say thank you to all the doctors, nurses, medical research
ers, and technicians. For their dedication, long hours, and pe\
sonal sacrifice. For their expertise. I say thank you to the dc
nor family for their compassion. But I give all the glory an\
praise to God. For without Him my story would not exist. Luc\
played no role in my life. The life changing experiences uniquel
affected me, but corporately my life changed many, many live\
I thank God for the privilege of being His instrument. I than\
God for Life.

Let everything that has breath praise the Lord.

Lord, thank You for my breath.

AMEN.

Hospital Stays

Nov. 2-4, 1994: Birth. St. Joseph's Hospital

Nov. 15, 1994 - Jan. 30, 1995: MCG (Heart surgery; severe ung problems)

Dec. 23, 1994: Trach

Jan. 30 - March 29, 1995: CHOP (Double lung transplant ind recovery)

March 29 - May 7, 1995: RMH

May 31, 1995: (Ear infection)

June 1-16, 1995: MCG (Multiple blood clots, dehydration)

June 25-29, 1995: CHOP (Rejection)

July 7, 1995: Good Dr.'s Appt. with Dr. Hudson

July 23, 1995: Face begins to swell

July 27 - Aug. 24, 1995: MCG (Blood clots, collection of un-known fluid in lungs)

Aug. 24 - Sept. 6, 1995: CHOP (Blood clots, Portacath)

Sept. 1, 1995: (G-tube placement)

Sept. 11-20, 1995: MCG (Severe breathing problems)

Sept. 22, 1995: MCG (Chest x-ray)

Sept. 25, 1995: MCG (Barium swallow/G.I. study for reflux)

Sept. 27-30, 1995: MCG (Started I.V. Hyperale, found lung :asts)

Dec. 3-22, 1995: CHOP (Scheduled lymphatic surgery--ulti-nately postponed)

Dec. 29, 1995 - Jan. 17, 1996: CHOP (SVC repair and open 1eart surgery)

Jan. 17-18, 1996: MCG (Twenty-four hour observation)

Jan. 21, 1996: Emergency room (respiratory distress)

Feb. 18-27, 1996: MCG (Flu, reactive airway disease)
Feb. 27 - March 5, 1996: CHOP (Infected portacath)
June 24, 1996: CHOP (Biopsy and routine "check-up")

EPILOGUE

Psalm 23 (KJV)
"The Lord is my shepherd; I shall not want. He maketh me to lie down in green pastures: he leadeth me beside the still waters. He restoreth my soul: he leadeth me in the paths of righteousness for his name's sake. Yea, though I walk through the valley of the shadow of death, I will fear no evil: for thou art with me; thy rod and thy staff they comfort me. Thou preparest a table before me in the presence of mine enemies: thou anointest my head with oil; my cup runneth over. Surely goodness and mercy shall follow me all the days of my life: and I will dwell in the house of the Lord forever."

Joshua was kind enough to share his story with us, and as his Granny, I tried to relate his life as unbiasedly as possible. If it became too granny-slated, please forgive me. The intent was to allow Joshua an open forum where he could communicate and educate. In order to obtain the latter, I would like to take this opportunity to give a few tips to the many wonderful people who want to help families like Joshua's, but aren't sure what to do.

1.) Please send cards. Cards are an excellent way to let the patient and his family know you care without intruding. They can be opened whenever it is convenient for the recipient, and they can be appreciated long afterward.

2.) If you feel you must call, please do not add any obligation and stress to the family. Many families leave an updated

message on their answering machine so the caller can find ou
the condition of the patient. Do not leave a phone number im
plying you expect a return call. And please--pass the progress
on to others so the phone does not ring constantly and perhaps
wake the patient.

3.) Respect the privacy of the family. NEVER just drop in a
the hospital or at home unless specifically requested to do so
Visiting takes energy. And NEVER bring your small children
They often are the source of dangerous germs.

4.) If the patient is a child, refrain from making reference to
healthy children, as this can deepen the family's feeling of loss.

5.) Don't minimize what is happening. Don't equate a situ
ation you may have experienced with what the family is dealing
with. No two illnesses are the same, and no two people have
the same feelings even in comparable situations.

6.) Be a listener--allow the caregiver the freedom to vent frus
tration, without trying to solve the situation. Validate the feel
ings, and above all, don't complain about situations that seem
trivial to someone facing long-term problems.

7.) When bringing food--which is always appreciated--use
disposable dishes, and please bring everything including nap
kins, plastic utensils, paper plates, and cups.

8.) Above all, please realize the family is stressed to the maxi
mum. Forgive what you may consider to be thoughtlessness or
ungrateful attitudes. For the majority of chronically ill patients
and their families, the wear and tear of daily living--not to men
tion the medical situation itself--drains everyone associated with
it. This is a time to be forgiving, faithful, and forever in prayer.

Thank you for all your support, concern, and love.

In His service,

Merrily (Granny) Bittler

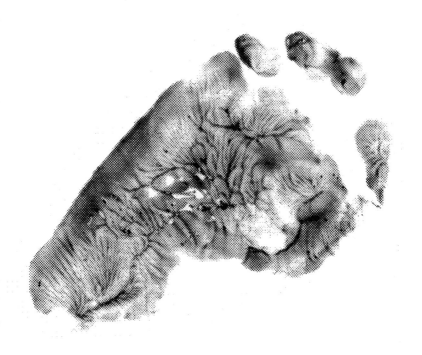

"A Typical Day at Home"

written by Traci (Mommy) Richardson

As usual, the alarm clock rings and wakes me up at 8:00 a.m. Every day starts no later than 8:00 a.m. for us because Joshua needs his first round of medicines. I go into Joshua's room to find him sleeping soundly. He's always been a great "sleeper" and I hate to awaken him but he needs to take his eight morning medications (cyclosporine, zantac, lasix, cisapride, bactrim, vitamin, nystatin, KCL) before their levels get too low in his bloodstream. Next, I give him a ten minute breathing treatment that helps open his airways so he can breathe easier. I take his temperature and check the oxygen level in his bloodstream (via a pulse oximeter probe I attach to his toe) to make sure everything checks out A-OK. Since Joshua hasn't learned to speak yet and tell me things like "mommy, I don't feel good" or "mommy, my head is hot", I have to rely on this important information to let me know if there may be an infection or rejection episode brewing. I change his diaper making sure to weigh it so I can keep track of how much fluid Joshua takes in and how much fluid comes out. Joshua loves to drink water and if I give him too much during the day or night, his already damaged kidneys have a hard time compensating and the excess fluid causes him to go into respiratory distress.

As I push each medicine diligently into Joshua's G-tube, I recite to him what I am doing. "The zantac is for the ulcer you get from the steroids you must take as a transplant patient. The lasix is for the kidney damage resulting from the anti-rejection medicine we give you. The cisapride helps the reflux you have from the G-tube feedings. The bactrim prevents pneumonia which you can't fight yourself because we keep you immuno-suppressed. The nystatin prevents thrush which your body also can't defend from properly because of the lack of an immune system. The KCL is an electrolyte that is needed because the lasix causes an imbalance of fluids. The vitamins you get because you are, after all a Baby." The cyclosporine is the only medicine Joshua must take by mouth.

By now it's 9:00 a.m. and we expect our daily phone call from Granny. The phone call comes right on time and as I let Granny know how Joshua is doing, I'm busily getting Joshua's feed pump and feed bag ready for "breakfast". Joshua's "breakfast", "lunch", and "dinner", consists of a 5-1/2 ounce serving of liquid PediaSure (with fiber) pumped through a stomach tube into his stomach. It takes approximately 45 minutes to pump all of the PediaSure into Joshua and we're both forced to sit very still during his feedings since the tubing only allows 24 inches of movement in any one direction away from the pump. I do my best to keep Joshua playing with stationary toys during his feedings but, you know how kids are....always wanting to go, go, go. I'm thankful when "breakfast" is over so I can start getting on with my day.

It's 10:00 a.m. now and I've just finished cleaning out his feed bag and hanging it up to dry. (We can't afford to let any bacteria grow in Joshua's equipment so I'm very diligent in cleaning and disinfecting everything). I take Joshua back to my bathroom and let him play with his favorite multi-colored ball while I take a quick shower. I finish getting dressed, make the beds, straighten up Joshua's room and the living room and turn on the T.V. just in time for Joshua's favorite show - The Price Is Right. He loves the beginning of the show when all of the contestants "come on down" and he actually claps when Bob Barker is introduced. He's no doubt Bob's #1 Fan!!

Now it's time to get outside and get some fresh air. Unfortunately, Georgia weather is not very cooperative when it comes to enjoying the great outdoors. Even the healthy population is struggling to breathe the thick, humid air and it's next to impossible to bring Joshua outside most of the time. So, instead, I pack him and his portable oxygen tank into the car and on good days we drive around between 11:30 a.m. and 2:00 p.m. We'll stop at a drive-thru for my lunch. Joshua loves his car rides and I love the fact that I can usually count on some peace and quiet while he takes a 40-minute nap in the back seat. Today, however, I need to make our trip a short one because we're expecting one of his three therapists to come to our house for a one hour session. They each come once a week.

Joshua and I pull into the driveway at 12:55 p.m. and patiently wait for the therapist. She shows up an hour late because there was a department store sale that she couldn't resist. Guess she thinks our world revolves around her...... uggh!! I assist during the hour long therapy session and Joshua works very hard as usual. The therapist leaves at 3:00 p.m. and I now have to hook Joshua up to the feeding pump again for another 45 minute feeding. I review the list of four "homework items" the therapist has left with me to work on during the next seven days. I start to get a headache trying to figure out when I'm going to do these extra exercises with Joshua in addition to the other exercises and medical requirements already placed on me by Joshua's two other therapists and his multiple doctors. No time to worry now. Joshua needs some more medicine.

I give him his 3:00 p.m. medicine (lasix, steroid, KCL) and entertain him while waiting for his feeds to finish. By 4:00 p.m. I've disconnected the feeding tube, re-washed the feed bag, changed/weighed another diaper, and finished giving him his second breathing treatment. I'm starting to get a little tired but realize that I have to start dinner. Joshua comes into the kitchen with me and plays with his refrigerator magnets while I cook something for my husband, Mason. I decide to get some laundry done before 5:30 p.m. when I'll need to leave to teach my aerobics class at the local YMCA. I've just started the laundry when the phone rings. I haven't answered the phone yet today because I've been a tad busy but, as I pick up the phone, I notice I have 5 phone messages that will need to be returned sometime. The person on the phone is in charge of scheduling a nurse to come stay with Joshua between 5:30 p.m. and 7:00 p.m. on Monday, Wednesday, and Friday while I teach aerobics. She has some bad news that she hopes "won't inconvenience me....today's nurse won't be able to come watch Joshua". She's got to be kidding!!! What am I supposed to do now??! Mason has already told me he has to work late (besides, his office is one hour away from our house and he'd never make it home in time to cover for the nurse!), I can't find a substitute for my aerobics class at this late hour, I can't take Joshua with me because he can't be around people, and I have 30 minutes to figure this mess out. You'd think I'd be prepared for this since it's not the first time the nurses have left me in a lurch but I keep hoping that one day they'll handle it more professionally. I put in a frantic call to my in-laws who, fortunately, are home and able to drop everything to rush over and help. I'm a nervous wreck all through my aerobics class because my in-laws aren't trained to handle a medical crisis, but as I arrive home at 7:15 p.m., I see that God has taken good care of the situation and everyone is fine.

Joshua has just finished his third tube feeding for the day and Mason and I sit down to eat the dinner I prepared earlier. We try to catch up on each other's day since this is the only 45 minutes we'll have together before it's medicine time for Joshua and things get hectic again. At 8:00 p.m. Mason gives Joshua his cyclosporine, imuran, zantac, and nystatin while I clean up the dinner dishes and fill up Joshua's portable oxygen tank for our daily evening walk. It's cooled down enough for Joshua to take a 30 minute walk with us around the neighborhood block. At Joshua's insistence, Mason and I take turns singing him his favorite songs, <u>Twinkle Twinkle Little Star</u>, <u>Old McDonald's Farm</u>, <u>The Wheels On The Bus</u>, and <u>The Baseball Song</u> while we push his stroller through the neighborhood.

We're back in our house between 8:30 and 9:00 p.m. - just in time to get Joshua ready for his bath. I'm usually in charge of bathtime and Mason helps by being the entertainment for Joshua. Once we have Joshua all cleaned up and in his pajamas, it's Mason's turn to check Joshua's evening vital signs. I head to the kitchen again to clean the medicine syringes, boil some more water for Joshua, since it's unsafe for him to drink tap water and he's used up the supply I had, and get his evening feed bag filled. At 9:30 p.m., Joshua gets his last dose of cisapride and lasix for the day and Mason begins to rock and sing him to sleep. By 10:00 p.m. Joshua is usually asleep in his crib and I am able to hook up his night feed which will run for the next 8 hours.

It's time now to think about tomorrow and I put together Mason's breakfast and lunch (provided I've had time to grocery shop and we actually have food in the house). Joshua's medications for the next 24 hours are drawn up and Mason and I begin to get ourselves ready for bed. At 11:00 p.m., Mason gives Joshua his last breathing treatment and last dose of KCL and crawls into bed. Although Joshua usually sleeps through most of the night, Mason and I alternate getting up to see why the feed pump alarm and/or the pulse oximeter alarm have gone off. We "fix" whatever has malfunctioned and drag ourselves back to bed. The next alarm I hear is <u>my</u> alarm clock.....it's 8 a.m. and another day!

"A Day in the Hospital"

written by Traci (Mommy) Richardson

If you've never spent at least 24 hours in a hospital, you don't know what you're missing. Allow me to take you through an average hospital day for me and Joshua....

At 5:30 a.m., we receive our first "visit" of the day from the x-ray technician. He noisily rolls in the portable x-ray machine and announces in a loud voice that it's time for Joshua's x-ray. No big deal EXCEPT Joshua is asleep - make that WAS asleep. I haven't seen the technician wash his hands so I question him. He gives me a perturbed look, admits he didn't wash his hands upon entering Joshua's **isolation** room, and shuffles over to the sink. Hand washing completed, Joshua and all of his miscellaneous lines are picked up so an x-ray film can be placed underneath him. I remind the technician to put a lead shield over Joshua's "privates" and bite my tongue as I think "why can't he ever remember to use that darn shield?!" I'm asked to step out of the room for a few minutes until the x-ray is completed. When I step back into the room, my first concern is to try to get Joshua back to sleep so he'll be as well-rested as possible for his long day of testing, surgery, and/or plain old recovery. Getting him quieted down after such a rude awakening is quite a challenge but within the hour I've got Joshua peacefully sleeping again. Make that WAS....it's now 7:00 a.m. and time for the nursing shifts to change.

More noise and disturbances that no one can sleep through. Our new nurse is responsible for getting Joshua's morning blood work. Since Joshua now has a portacath placed just under the skin, the nurse has a direct line for her blood draw. The problem is that she isn't familiar with the procedure necessary to access a portacath so she goes in search of an "expert". The "expert" arrives and I'm in charge of holding Joshua's arms and upper body still while the "expert" sterilizes the skin, accesses the portacath, and fills up the necessary vials with blood. Joshua hates being held down and feels the needle as it pierces his skin. He's crying hard but I can't soothe him until the procedure is done. After a long 15-20 minutes, the needle is removed and I do what I can to stop Joshua's tears.

Now it's time to administer Joshua's first round of medications. He gets seven different medications at 8:00 a.m.. I push five of them into his G-tube and the other two Joshua has to take orally. He moves his head away from the medicine syringe I'm trying to squirt into his mouth....you would too if you tasted these two medications. One is so sweet it's nauseating and the other one is so bitter you can't get rid of the taste for hours. After a moderate struggle, I manage to get all of the medicines into Joshua.

A respiratory therapist comes in to make sure I have all of the necessary items for Joshua's morning breathing treatment. Before I can answer, a medical student wanders in and asks how Joshua's night was. I give her the update, she does a quick examination of Joshua, and she's gone. Back to the respiratory therapist.....yes, I have everything I need. He leaves and I complete the 10 minute breathing treatment.

The nurse comes back and completes her assessment of Joshua while I get his morning feeding of PediaSure ready. Of course, I have to remind her, too, to wash her hands. There are signs up all around Joshua's room requiring strict hand washing to reduce the chance of bringing any germs in to Joshua, yet very few of the medical staff bother to take the time to wash.....just one more reason to stay on my toes!! As exhausted as I am, I force myself to stay alert to everyone coming and going out of Joshua's room so that NO ONE touches my baby without washing the germs off of their hands first.   Joshua finishes his tube feeding and I disconnect the feeding bag and clean it out so it's ready for lunch time.

It's time for me to get myself showered and dressed. I leave the "watch duty" to Mason or Granny (whoever happens to be helping me out at the moment) and I run up to the fifth floor of the hospital where there is a shower room. I take a quick shower, get dressed, and get back to Joshua's room ASAP. I hate leaving Joshua even for a minute because a lot of human medical error can happen very quickly and I feel 100% responsible for making sure no one makes any more mistakes on Joshua that will cost him his health or add one more minute to his hospital stay.

I continue to give Joshua his medications, breathing treatments, and feeds throughout the day. I've finally proven my ability as care-giver to the hospital staff (after many months) and they stay out of Joshua's room most of the day except for an occasional "pop-in" to check Joshua's vital signs. We have a visit from the physical therapist who tries to get Joshua to work his muscles a little bit but he's not feeling well enough to cooperate. Since the physical therapist adds one more source for germs AND Joshua clearly seems to be disinterested in the activities, I request that the sessions be discontinued. I need to do what's best for Joshua, and, right now, it's to get him healthy enough to get him OUT of the hospital. We'll worry about his muscles later!

It's lunch time for all of us. Joshua eats through his G-tube as usual and Mason (or Granny) runs down to the hospital cafeteria for a sandwich. We eat lunch at Joshua's bedside - if we're in Philadelphia that is. One of the worst hospital rules I've come across is the "no eating in a patient's room" rule. I'm sure the hospital staff is trying to encourage parents to get out of their child's room to get some nourishment, some fresh air, and renewed energy but what they end up accomplishing is having exhausted parents skip crucial meals instead of having to be apart from their seriously ill child. Stupid!! The only other hospital rule that is worse than the no eating rule is the "no parents/visitors" rule. The theory behind this rule is to have the patient's room cleared out for an hour during shift change so there isn't alot of distraction for the nurses while they're giving and receiving medical reports. Well, take it from a parent, you'll need to come up with a much more important reason than shift change to get me to leave my baby's side. Besides, if they're so busy giving medical reports to the new nurse who the heck is watching Joshua??!!

As the day progresses, I get ready for at least one, if not all, of Joshua's doctors to stop in, by writing down all of my medical questions for the day. The doctors finally make their rounds in the early evening and I fire my list of questions at them. They're able to answer some but not all of the questions. They just can't explain what is going on with Joshua - not very comforting.

I give Joshua a sponge bath as we prepare for bedtime. I long for the day I don't have to use a sponge to carefully wash around all of Joshua's sterile lines. One of these days he's going to have a real bath!! I change the sheets on Joshua's crib and dress him in a yellow hospital gown. Not very attractive but we're in no position to be choosey. We turn off the lights in the room but it's still fairly bright from the light at the nurse's station. It's also still noisy as monitors beep, doctors are paged, phones are ringing, and babies are crying. If we waited for peace and quiet before we went to bed, we'd never even get to close our eyes. We all do our best to tune out the hospital hubbub.

The night nurse awakens me every other hour when she comes in to check Joshua's blood pressure and temperature. I'm sure she keeps Joshua from getting a good night's rest but no matter how many times I try to have this ritual changed, I never succeed. *"It's hospital policy"* I'm told.

My frustration grows with every day and every night as I see complete loss of privacy, the lack of any decision-making opportunities, negligent hand washing practices, medication errors, blood drawing mistakes, violation of sterile procedures, etc. And yet, these medical professionals are trying to get my son healthy enough to go home and, for that, I'm grateful. Just know this, if I never see another hospital again, I'll be the happiest mother around!!

Collection of Letters

November 22, 1995

Dear Brothers and Sisters in Christ, (in Cuba and in Brazil)

As we celebrate Thanksgiving Day here in the States, I want each of you to know how very thankful I am for you, your love, and your prayers. I will never be able to fully express the blessings you are to me. Receiving your letters and kind words fills my heart with gladness and gratitude. Thank you.

And a special thank you for your prayers and concern for Joshua. Did you know that the word "Joshua" literally translated means "Jesus saves"? And so He has for the last year and 20 days. Joshua celebrated his 1st birthday on Nov. 2, 1995 and was baptized just three days later in a Presbyterian Church in Augusta, Georgia. There is a huge significance to his baptism since he is not allowed around people for fear he will pick up a germ. He has no immune system because of all the medicines he takes to keep his body from rejecting his new lungs. Even a common cold could kill him. But God protected Joshua as He has for so long, and we are humbled by His Mercy!

Next week Joshua will once again go to Philadelphia, Pennsylvania for more surgery. He has a technical problem with his lymph system which prevents his body from absorbing his food. The substitute food the doctors are feeding him is destroying his liver. We pray for God's strength and for His grace as we endure yet another life threatening surgery. All praise and glory be to God the Father and His Son, Jesus.

I would like to take this opportunity to wish you a Blessed Christmas and a New Year that brings you closer to our Beloved Savior. You are now and will always be in my thoughts and prayers.

With much love through Christ,
Merrily

December 23, 1995

Dear Friends and Family,

Merry Christmas! Wow, it's hard to imagine that yet another year has passed, but we just celebrated Joshua's one-year birthday (<u>out</u> of the hospital!) on November 2nd, so we know the end of 1995 is fast approaching! We have had quite a year but we'll save that for a little later. For now, I want to thank each and every one of you for your prayers and support over the past many months. Whether you know it or not, God has used each of you in a very special way in our lives and we are forever grateful. Before you read on, please keep in mind that this year was a time of trials for our family BUT it was also a time to see first-hand how God has worked miracles through Joshua from the very first day he was hospitalized so . . . keep a smile on your face and a prayer of thankfulness on your lips.

January found us sitting in the Intensive Care Unit in Augusta, Georgia faced with the decision of whether to pursue a double lung transplant for 2-month old Joshua. He would be the fifth infant <u>ever</u> to undergo such a surgery and there were no medical statistics to indicate any degree of success, however, there really was no other option available to us so the decision was made to go to Philadelphia for the transplant. We arrived in Philadelphia on Monday, January 30th and Joshua underwent many tests and screenings in the next 24 hours to begin the process of "matching" him to a donor organ <u>if</u> and when one became available. We had been warned that the wait for a pair of donor lungs would take months or longer. Well, God had other plans. On February 1st, **less than 24 hours after Joshua had been officially listed as a lung transplant recipient,** our cardiologist came to Joshua's room and announced that a pair of donor lungs had become available. They were as close to a perfect match as we could ask for! Joshua was wheeled into surgery at 7 p.m. and at 11:30 p.m. the transplant was completed and Joshua was back in his room. He looked like he had challenged Mike Tyson to a fight and LOST but God had brought him through a rare and complex surgery alive!

The next three months were spent in the Philadelphia Hospital battling infections and weight gain problems and strengthening Joshua's weak abdominal muscles so he could expand his new lungs and breathe without a ventilator. Mason was travelling back and forth from Augusta to Philadelphia so he could spend every non-working minute with us on the weekends and my mother, "Granny," took over the weekday duty when Mason had to head back to work. Meanwhile, I officially hung up my engineering hat with Westinghouse and took on the role of full-time mom. (By the way, did you know that moms don't get any vacation time, weekends, or overtime pay??!! Whew, what an eye opener yet what a blessing when you can spend every minute with your beautiful baby.)

On May 6th, after 96 days in Philadelphia (but who's counting?), we loaded Joshua and all our belongings into a rental van and headed HOME to Georgia. It was a <u>LONG</u> 15-hour trip, but at least we were going South. Once we got back to Georgia, we had to adjust to our new "transplant lifestyle." Joshua was taking 13 medications seven different times throughout the day. He was being fed through a tube in his nose in the hopes of getting him to gain weight. He was getting four 10-minute respiratory treatments a day to help his breathing, and the list goes on and on. Thankfully, God gave "Dr. Traci" and "Dr. Mason" the stamina we needed to tackle this new challenge. Oh yeah, I almost forgot to mention that we earned our medical degree during all of this. It only took us six months of living in hospitals and, frankly, I don't know why it takes all the other doctors-to-be almost ten years. They must be slow learners! (Just kidding, Tammi and Mike.) We also could not (and still can't) take Joshua around people because three of his medications significantly lower his ability to fight infections and people are a huge source of germs/infections. One of these days in the not too distant future we hope to be able to get out a little more with Joshua, but in the meantime, you'll have to take the word of two very non-biased (ha!) parents that our little Joshua is the most beautiful little boy. (Check out our Christmas picture and judge for yourselves!)

By June 1st (only three short weeks after our return trip from Philly), Joshua started having more medical difficulties. He developed a serious blood clot in his right chest/neck area which has subsequently led to even more serious and complicated lymphatic problems. (See, now you're the one getting a crash course in anatomy.) From June through October, Joshua was hospitalized repeatedly in Georgia and flown to Philadelphia twice. He continues to have complications with his lymphatic system as a result of the first blood clot. In fact, we just got back from a three week stay in Philadelphia hospital where we tried to work through the latest problem but it sill looks like we may have a tough road ahead of us. We were fortunate, however, to have had the opportunity to spend a wonderfully quiet and relatively relaxed Thanksgiving--in our new home. We actually found a spare minute (not two, mind you.) in between hospitalizations to make the big move into our first non-rental home. YEAH! We're still maneuvering around quite a few moving boxes, but that can be next year's project!

As you can see, there's never a dull moment in the Richardson household. The GREAT news is that God has been with us through our journey in '95--the good and thankfully, the bad times, too. He has changed our lives forever with Joshua and his medical problems. We may never know why He planned this for our family, but we do know that He is the provider of ALL things and He is forever faithful to His promises. We have been reminded of that daily as we turn to Him for strength, wisdom, and comfort, and that, my friends, has made 1995 a wonderful year!!!

Have a very Merry Christmas!

Love,
Traci, Mason, and Joshua

Christmas 1995

Dear Friends

1995 was not just another typical year for the Bittler family. Tammi and her husband Mike both entered private practices as full-fledged doctors and bought a beautiful house in Kennebunk, Maine. Traci and Mason also bought and moved into a new home in Georgia. Sandi has been travelling with the women's Olympic Basketball Team for the last three months. Ronnie moved into a new apartment in Maryland, and Robbie has taken on new responsibilities with his job in Ohio. Ron and I still take care of his Mom whose condition (Alzheimer patient) continues to disintegrate. But all this pales in comparison to what has occurred in Baby Joshua's life.

Traci and Mason's son, Joshua, just turned 13 months old. Last year at this time he was in a hospital in Georgia recuperating from heart surgery. This year he is at Children's Hospital of Philadelphia awaiting future surgery. In the past twelve months he has spent approximately ten months in either Georgia's or Philadelphia's hospital. There have been many surgeries but the most complicated was the double lung transplant he received on Feb. 1st. Our lives have been totally changed--financially, emotionally, physically, and spiritually. For many of you, I must say, "Thank you!" Thank you for your love and concern. Thank you for your faithful prayer support. We could never have come this far without you and without God's grace and mercy through His Son, Jesus Christ. For those of you who did not know about Joshua's battle for life, we just ask that you, too, keep him in your prayers.

And so as we celebrate Christmas this year, it is with renewed meaning and gratitude. A Baby was born almost 2000 years ago. And because of His birth we are blessed with the peace and joy of another baby--Baby Joshua.

May God touch your lives this Christmas season and during the New Year. And may you have a wonderful holiday.

Ron & Merrily Bittler and family

January 15, 1996

"Your kingdom come, your will be done on earth as it is in Heaven."

Matthew 6:10

While most of us went to New Year's Eve parties, Traci, Mason, and Joshua were aboard a medijet flying back to Children's Hospital of Philadelphia after being home for just one week. Once again Joshua was suffering from unknown complications. His breathing was difficult, his lung x-rays showed signs of problems, and his upper body (face, chest, arms) were swollen to at least three times his normal size.

On January 2, the cardiologist did a heart catheterization and discovered a constriction in Joshua's Superior Vena Cava. While attempting to fix it with a metal stent, the stent accidentally fell into Joshua's heart. Immediately open heart surgery was performed and the stent retrieved. Joshua's recovery from the surgery has been slowed by pneumonia and his inability to breathe without the ventilator. On one occasion he went into respiratory arrest.

I apologize for not writing individual letters to each of you. Your faithful prayer support has been a blessing to each of us. A simple "thank you" does not seem adequate in expressing our gratitude, but it conveys a heart full of appreciation and love from us.

I have spent all of 1996 in Philadelphia with Traci, Mason, and Joshua, and have returned to Mercer for a few days of "R&R." (Not rest and relaxation, but Ron and Ron's Mom!) We all survived the Blizzard of '96, watching the snow accumulate from our 6th floor window. Mason found the storm to be "exciting" since he's a Georgia native!

We know God's "Kingdom come, His will be done on earth as it is in Heaven." He has brought us this far. We will surely trust Him for the remainder of the journey.

Thank You,

Merrily Bittler

PS. To receive an update on Joshua's condition, please do not hesitate to call Trinity Presbyterian Church at 412-662-2680.

PPS. Joshua's home address is: 252 Bohler Dr., Evans, GA 30809

February 10, 1996

Dear family and friends,

Thank you so much for your love and concern these many months. Your prayers and cards have been a real blessing to me and also my Mommy and Daddy and even my Granny and Gramps. Oops--almost forgot--my Great Grandma Jean, too. We all are so grateful.

I continue to have both good days and bad days, but I never have a day that God isn't with me. He gives each one of us the strength we need to take one day at a time.

When I'm having a good day, I sit up and play "clap-clap" and peek-a-boo. I don't much like TV but there's one show I won't miss--The Price is Right. It's my very favorite. I have lots of toys but I enjoy playing with all the medical equipment I'm attached to. It's fun to see Mommy get upset when I pull off my oxygen and yank the tube in my tummy. She's pretty quick.

I also roll on the floor and wiggle around a lot. That way I can set monitors off and get all sorts of attention. Before my last heart surgery (1/2/96) I was standing up with lots of help. Now, I'm waiting for my physical therapist to bring me new exercises to strengthen my muscles again. While I wait, I've considered making Mommy really happy by eating the normal way. I mean, by mouth. But if I do then my twelve beautiful teeth will need to be brushed. I hate things in my mouth. All that yucky medicine I've taken all these months just kinda took all the fun out of "open, chew, and swallow." For now I'm just going to let the feeding tube do its thing. After all, I weigh almost 22 pounds.

In all modesty, though, I must say I'm a pretty cute little fellow. Most people love my big brown eyes and curly hair.

Mommy cut off a few curls last week after the Steelers lost the Super Bowl. Made me wonder if linebacker Kevin Green did the same. People also love the beautiful dimples I have. (Got 'em from my Daddy!) I smile lots and lots to show them off.

I'm not allowed to be around many people because of my suppressed immune system and germs and stuff, but--I do the neatest "hi-five" with all my family and my favorite doctors and nurses. If I really want to impress someone I blink my eyes. I haven't mastered a one-eyed wink quite yet. Of course, I haven't actually mastered eating and breathing quite yet either.

So in spite of all my medical problems, I'm a pretty neat kid. Mommy says I'm a KEEPER! Guess so. I keep all the doctors guessing, keep all my family exhausted, and keep all my friends praying. And all I can say is "Thanks!" Actually, I can't even say that 'cuz I don't really have a voice. But I think you know how I feel about all of you. I love you!

May God Bless You!

Joshua

PS. A note from Granny:

Joshua was flown from the hospital in Philadelphia to the hospital in Augusta Georgia on Jan. 17th. He was discharged the following day. He celebrated his one year "lung birthday" on Feb. 1, 1996 and his 15 month birthday on Feb. 2, 1996. Gramps and I visited him during that week. Please remember the donor's family in your prayers during this difficult time for them.

Love, Merrily

February 26, 1996

Dear Friends,

This Joshua update was prompted mainly because I've broken my ankle and have to rest for a few days. The optimum word being FEW! I have no intention of being laid up for long--just slowed down a little. Thankfully I'm in a walking cast.

Joshua once again is in the hospital. It started with a "flu" bug, but there is no way Joshua can handle any germ. It progressed to dehydration, blood clots in the subclavian, kidney malfunction, and respiratory distress. Then to complicate it, he got a blood infection and the lining of his heart became infected with a staph virus.

For the past week, Joshua has been in the Pediatric ICU in Georgia. The doctors there want to treat him (and are treating him) with antibiotics. The doctors in Philadelphia want Joshua to come to Philly and they do not want antibiotics used, but rather want to remove an object that is in Joshua's heart allowing access to obtain blood without repeatedly "sticking" him. Complicated? You bet.

Meanwhile we wait. If he goes to Philly I will go also. If he stays in Georgia, I'll stay in Mercer until he's discharged and then go help Traci.

We did reach a milestone. Joshua was out of the hospital for 29 consecutive days. The longest in his life. He also made some progress eating some food by mouth. He continues to amaze us with how bright he is. When the doctors and nurses have stayed in his room longer than he wants, he simply waves bye-bye until they get the drift! We're planning on teaching him tact in the near future.

Once again we thank you for your faithful prayers. We truly are blessed by our loving Heavenly Father and by each one of you.

Much love,
Merrily

PS. Don't get too used to these letters. I don't plan on making this a habit!

April 24, 1996
Two years from my visit

Dear Friends, (in Cuba)

I have written several letters but I am not sure if you received any of them since more restrictions have been put on travel by our government and some of the church groups decided not to risk a trip to your country.

Please know my thoughts and prayers are with you always, and that I long to hear from you and know how you are doing.

God continues to hear all your prayers and mine concerning Baby Joshua. As you can see by the photos, Joshua is growing although his medical condition remains uncertain and he will once again be hospitalized in Philadelphia on May 13th for surgery and tests. We are so grateful to you for your love and concern and to God for His everlasting strength, peace, and mercy.

In His Love and Service,

Merrily

Dear Friends,

It has been almost two months since my last update and I
apologize for the silence. Time has not stood still, only my pen.
Nor has Joshua stood still. He spent almost two weeks in
Children's Hospital of Philadelphia (CHOP). Traci and Mason
stayed with him the first week, and I stayed with him and Traci
the second week. It was truly amazing to observe his steady
progress daily as he continued to improve until he was finally
discharged and sent back to the hospital in Georgia. After only
one day there, he was allowed to go home where he has remained to this day.

The down side to this good news is that Joshua still requires
oxygen to breathe and the doctors cannot figure out why. And
so a biopsy must be performed on his lungs to determine if he
is in rejection. He is presently on high doses of steroids to treat
a reactive airway condition and possibly asthma. As he is
weaned from the steroids over the next six weeks he will be
ready for another trip to Philadelphia and his biopsy. Until we
get the results of the biopsy we will remain cautiously optimistic about his medical condition.

Our entire family has had an opportunity to visit Traci, Mason, and Joshua during the past three weeks. It has been wonderful to see first hand how well he interacts with all of us--just
as long as his Mommy stays VERY close. Once again we are
reminded of just how good God has been to allow us the privilege of having Joshua as our special baby. We feel just as privileged to have wonderful friends like you, who have faithfully
prayed and supported us for these many months. We hope that
we can someday repay in some small measure the gratitude we

feel. For in reality, Joshua is also your special baby too.

It is a relief to have no major crisis situations in the past six weeks, but please realize that Joshua's condition is fragile at all times and we hope that you will continue to pray for him daily as we continue to walk humbly as God directs us.

Thank you so much.

In the precious name of Jesus,

Merrily

PS. My ankle is out of the cast and I once again am walking without any help. PTL!!

June 15, 1996

Greetings to our wonderful prayer family,

What a blessing I experienced on a quick trip to Augusta to visit with Traci, Mason and Joshua for three days. I have never seen Joshua any happier or healthier and we just praise God and thank you for being such faithful prayer warriors! The trip ended way too soon but not before Joshua once again remembered who his Granny is. Although Joshua is not one to enjoy a lot of affection, he did allow me to hold him just so long as I didn't get too huggie/kissy! I tried my best to accommodate his rules.

Joshua is now 19 1/2 months old. He weighs 26 pounds and is 30 inches long. He continues to take 15 medicines daily some of which have affected his growth and we think may be the reason for his continuous upset stomach. He vomits several times a day. He eats only through his G-tube, but will drink water from his bottle. All other food by mouth makes him gag. He still needs oxygen at all times. BUT. . .

He sits alone. He's beginning to babble. He laughs out loud. He communicates by pointing, shaking his head no, clapping his hands for yes, and is very patient while we figure out what he wants. He rolls from one end of the room to the next (and looks like a ball of yarn when he's done.) Oh, he also jumps in his jumpy seat and swings in his swing!

On June 19th Joshua will return to Philly for his lung biopsy and other possible tests including a heart catheterization. We request that your prayers for Joshua increase during that critical time. Also, perhaps you could include his parents as this continual stress is taking its toll on their relationship.

With grateful hearts for the past and joyful expectation for the future, we remain steadfast in the Love of Christ.

Merrily

June 21, 1996

My dearest friends, [in Cuba]

I received many letters from you and I want to thank you so much. It is always very uplifting to me to hear from you and to know that you are continuing to pray for Joshua and my family. Many, many thanks. I want you to know that you also are in my daily prayers. I miss and love each one of you.

The saying goes "A picture is worth 1,000 words." I hope that these pictures let you see for yourself how God has blessed Joshua. (And also me--my broken ankle is fine. My husband's injuries from the car accident are all healed also.) Joshua is now 19 1/2 months old. He weights 26 pounds and is 30 inches long. That is very small for his age, but it is one of the known side effects of some of the 15 medicines he takes daily. He still eats nothing by mouth and his oxygen requirement is constant. Next week he will return to Philadelphia to see if perhaps his body is rejecting his lungs. We pray this is not the case.

I recently spent three days in Georgia with Joshua and my daughter and son-in-law. I was so blessed to be able to interact with Joshua. He is a very happy baby, but not one for being hugged and kissed. But he even let me do that. I praise God for His everlasting love, grace, and mercy. "He is our Rock and our Refuge." Thank You Jesus!

It is my prayer that each of you are healthy and are remaining steadfast in your walk with our Lord. May He continue to give you joy, peace, and hope as He directs your paths and may we all realize that we all serve the same risen Savior--Jesus Christ.

In His name and in His love, I remain as always yours,

Merrily

August 14, 1996

Greetings from Georgia.

It's time to update all of my wonderful friends and family and thank you for continuing to pray for me. I am overwhelmed and most appreciative of your love, support, and concern. You have been a blessing to me and my Mommy and Daddy.

As you can see by the photos I'm putting on a few pounds. And a little hair. The "button" on my tummy is how I'm still fed. My diet consists of PediaSure (in case any of you want to gain weight) and it's pumped into my stomach three times a day, and almost continually during the night. I wish the tubing from the pump to my button was longer because it dramatically curtails my range of movement.

In case you aren't aware of my mobility--I can really MOVE! I roll amazingly well--with speeds yet to be determined but close to the approved speed limits set by the Georgia Highway Patrol. I can visit Mommy and Daddy in any room in our house. They were so smart to get a house all on one level. And I'm smart enough to unravel all the oxygen tubing once I arrive at my destination. It takes quite some time and concentration, but I'm mastering the art.

I'm also beginning to crawl, but it's so much more work than rolling and a lot slower. I'm thinking about walking but that looks even harder than crawling. I can use my walker and I love my bouncy seat and swing.

My extra body hair is a result of my anti-rejection medicine. The doctors in Philadelphia were surprised to see me "fuzzy" and have now changed me to a different anti-rejection medicine. I'll probably go bald (on my body, not my head) just in time for winter and I'll miss my furry coat.

Hopefully I'll spend all winter in warm Georgia and out of the hospital. I'll adjust to smooth arms and legs!

My trip to Philadelphia was better than anyone hoped. All my tests were good. I came down from seventeen medicines daily to fourteen, and the best news is there will be no more routine biopsies--only when I'm showing signs of real rejection. Dr. Spray said he no longer considers me to be a "fragile" baby and he gave Mommy permission to take me "out and about" as long as I don't come in contact with a lot of people.

So--the first place I went was to visit my Granny and Gramps in Mercer. The trip went okay, but the weather was so hot and humid, I almost melted and I was happy to get back in an air-conditioned house. I've also gone for lots of walks in my stroller, to the bank, TCBY (watched Mommy and Granny pig out) and to a few non-crowded stores. I'm amazed at what I've missed all these months!

Did you know I now have a voice? I can say Ma-ma and a few more things Mommy and Daddy don't quite understand yet. I'm sure they'll grasp it soon.

I'm learning sign language also, so I can communicate quite well. "No" is still my most effective sign--I can really shake my head. "Yes" is not a nod, but rather I clap my hands. Pointing also works well.

I blow kisses, will give a hug, can tell you my age (1 finger), know all my body parts, can "talk" on the phone--even dialed once (the wrong number)--and am a wealth of information if only I'm asked the right questions. I love music, books, and bath time. But most of all I love God My Creator, Jesus my Savior, the Holy Spirit my Protector, and you!

JOSHUA